52 DRAMATIC MOMENTS
FOR WORSHIP AND MINISTRY

Compiled by Matt Tullos
and Christy Marsh Haines

PHOTOCOPY RIGHTS INCLUDED

ACKNOWLEDGEMENTS

Scripture quotations marked *AMP* are from *The Amplified New Testament*
© The Lockman Foundation 1954, 1958, 1987. Used by permission.

Scripture quotations marked *KJV* are from the *King James Version* of the Bible.

Scripture quotations marked *NASB* are from the *New American Standard Bible*.
© The Lockman Foundation, 1960, 1962, 1963, 1968, 1971, 1972, 1973, 1975, 1977.
Used by permission.

Scripture quotations marked *NIV* are taken from the Holy Bible, *New International Version*,
copyright © 1973, 1978, 1984 by International Bible Society.

Scripture quotations marked *NKJV* are from The Holy Bible, *New King James Version*,
Copyright © 1982, 1983, 1985 by Thomas Nelson, Inc., Publishers.

Scripture quotations marked *NRSVB* are taken from the *New Revised Standard Version of the
Bible*, copyright ©1989 by the Division of Christian Education of the National Council
of Churches of Christ in the United States of America.
Used by permission. All rights reserved.

Scripture references marked *TLB* are taken from *The Living Bible*.
Copyright Tyndale House Publishers, Wheaton, Illinois, 1971. Used by permission.

Copyright 1995
Reprinted 1997
Church Street Press
ISBN 0-8054-9814-1
Photocopy Rights Included

52 Dramatic Moments for Ministry
Dewey Decimal Classification: 812
Subject Heading: Public Worship-Drama-Collections

Printed in the United States of America

Genevox Music Group
127 Ninth Avenue North
Nashville, TN 37234

INTRODUCTION

DRAMATIC MOMENTS FLOOD THE SCRIPTURE. Moments of triumph, exaltation, fear, disbelief, and stark realization. Moments that have changed the course of history. Moments that have altered the direction of millions of lives. Moments created by the reality of One Life. The Life of Jesus. What's your favorite dramatic moment in scripture? Here's one of mine: It was like a press conference without microphones. As Jesus and the disciples (turned theologians) passed by a blind beggar, they began the search for someone to blame. "Who caused this blind man to lose his sight? Was it sin? Who sinned? The father or the mother? Or did *he* sin? He was born blind, but, perhaps God in His all-knowing judgement, knew that he was going to perpetrate some horrible sin and just decided to mete out the punishment *before* the fact."

I can feel Jesus' frustration. I can imagine the blind man overhearing the discussion, listening very intently because this is a question that he has asked all his life. Now, finally, the answer would come.

Jesus is about to speak, but, as he opens His mouth, Peter starts in again, "Was this because his parents had sinned?" No, Peter. "Did he sin?" No, Thomas. "Well, why did it happen?" "Why do these things happen?" "Did his mother have a disease?" "Does God hate his family?" "Did he injure himself as a baby?"

Finally Jesus had had enough! I imagine that in Judean vernacular He said, "Hold it! Your questions aren't important. You're looking for someone to blame. I'm looking for someone to heal! We don't have time to have a seminar on human suffering. He's blind and, in case you've forgotten, I'm Jesus! Let's give this man some sight! I'm not going to be here very long. We could discuss this until the cows come home, but this beggar would still be blind."

Jesus stooped down and made clay. That would really make the Pharisees mad.

Then He put the clay on the beggar's eyes. They wouldn't like that, either.

He told the beggar to go wash the goop off at the local pool, Siloam. And, as always, Jesus did the impossible. The beggar could see!

This leads us to the self-righteous tattletales of the first century. The people were amazed for a moment or two then they said, "Wait till the Pharisees hear about this one!" And, of course, they went directly to the big shots. Can you imagine the redness in their faces when they were told about this miracle. The redness of righteous indignation is neither righteous nor dignified. "He did a miracle on the Sabbath. Doesn't He know that miracles aren't supposed be happening on the Sabbath?!"

What a strange and comical story! It would be even funnier if it wasn't true today. But, the fact is, churches still choose philosophy over ministry. We're more concerned about why bad things happen than how good things are born from bad things. We find comfort in parameters. And we are extremely fearful that miraculous things might happen on the Lord's Day.

While a majority of us are vainly practicing our ritualistic, self-righteous two-step in three-four time accompanied by organ and piano, there is a Man spitting in the dirt, making clay, and opening eyes. His name is Jesus.

This book is a collection of mud pies which we hope will open the eyes of the world to the radical grace of the Father. Visualize this incredible message of grace — and may the blind receive sight!

—Matt

TABLE OF CONTENTS

THE TRIAL OF CHRIST
by Stephen R. Poole

Try this great worship and discussion sketch!

Cast:
Judge (choir director if using with music)
Mr. (or **Miss**) **Night** *(prosecuting attorney — charismatic, handsome, devilish person)*
Judas *(haggard, crazed, wearing biblical costume)*
Mr. (or **Miss**) **Black** *(uneducated, rough, business type)*
Satan *(angelic, handsome, intelligent, crafty)*

Setting: *Court room with judge's stand center stage (pulpit); witness seat beside that; attorney's table at an angle, so face is visible to audience.*

Judge: This is a rather unusual case. For over 2000 years, people have been debating if the man known as Jesus Christ was the true Son of God or just some crazy lunatic. Today I have been charged with the task of making a decision as to just who Jesus Christ of Nazareth was, and what his real intentions were so many years ago. I was informed that there will be no defense attorney present today, so we will hold any witnesses for the defense until last. Mr. Night, you may begin with the prosecution.

Night: Thank you, Your Honor. I think it is obvious what the outcome of today's proceedings will be. The people of the world have voiced their opinions against this man Jesus. We plan to prove that Jesus was not only a fake, but that He knowingly led thousands, perhaps millions, of people to believe His teachings when He had no way of fulfilling any of His promises. This Jesus who, by the way, is not even here on His own behalf, has lied to and cheated men, women, and even children for about 2000 years now. It is the desire of the people that

He be found to be nothing more than the common crook that He is, and that this court order Him to cease any and all teachings about Himself. *(pause)* For my first witness I would like to call on a man who knew that Jesus was a traitor to His own people, and traveled closely with Jesus for over two years — Judas Iscariot. *(Judas takes the stand)* Judas, tell us in your own words what kind of man this Jesus of Nazareth was.

Judas: He was a crazy man, that's what He was. Even His mother thought so. She and her other sons came to a house where we were one day and tried to get Jesus to go home with them. She said He was going to get Himself killed, the way He was carrying on. Not only was He crazy, but He was a lawbreaker also. He knew it was wrong to work on the Sabbath, but He did . . . healing, picking wheat, and telling men to pick up their bedrolls and go home after He healed them. And He also was a blasphemer. He called Himself God's Son. His own teachings weren't consistent with His actions. He taught that we should look after the poor, yet when Mary was chastised for wasting precious perfume that could have been sold to help the poor, Jesus said that she was right to show her attention to Him. He said that we would always have the poor with us, but that He would only be with us for a short time. You see, He wanted us to serve Him.

Night: Did you know that the religious leaders wanted to capture Jesus?

Judas: Yes. I told them that I would help them capture Him. After all, they offered me 30 pieces of silver.

Night: I understand that you committed suicide, Judas. Why?

Judas: After I saw His face when I kissed it and looked into His eyes, I knew instantly that He had known all along that I was going to turn Him over to the authorities. He used me from the beginning so that He could begin His twisted war. He knew that His death would bring about a rallying of the Jewish people. I couldn't stand having been used like that.

Night: Thank you, that will be all. (*Judas leaves the stand.*) For the people's second witness we call Tracy Black. (**Black** *enters.*) Mr. Black, would you please tell the court about yourself.

Black: I am a self-made millionaire. I own several companies which deal with various products and services. The two largest are my beer company and a chain of abortion clinics.

Night: Have you ever met the defendant, Mr. Black?

Black: Well, not personally . . . but I was raised by my aunt and she said that she had met Him personally.

Night: What kind of person was your aunt?

Black: Aunt Bess was a crazy, senile, old lady. She would dance around the house singing and talking to herself. She would work hard all day sewing dresses for the rich ladies and then give most of it away to that church she made me attend.

Night: Against your will?

Black: Yeah! I certainly didn't want to go, but she said that Jesus would be mad if I stayed home.

Night: What were the people like there?

Black: Where?

Night: At the church.

Black: Oh, well . . . they were all weird.

Night: What do you mean "weird"?

Black: They were completely different in church than they were during the week. Most partied every Friday but talked about how bad it was when they were at church on Sunday.

Night: Why are you now speaking out against the defendant?

Black: He's ruining my business. I've worked hard to get a good income and now I'm at a standstill. My profits haven't grown any for several months now. I wanted to start selling vending machines that would automatically dispense my beer, like soda machines, but His followers have thrown a fit about it and now the court has ruled against me. And you know the situation with abortion clinics and those radicals that would rather go to jail than to let my customers get through without being harassed.

Night: And because of this you feel that your income has suffered?

Black: Sure it has. They ought to mind their own business.

Night: That will be all, Mr. Black. Thank you. *(Black leaves.)* My next witness is the only one that can describe to us exactly what it is that Jesus has been doing to deceive people. I call on Lucifer, whom many know as Satan. *(Satan takes the stand.)* Would you please tell us what Jesus has been doing to deceive people for the past 2000 years?

Satan: It started much further back than that. It began with God. You see, God was this powerful being who was bored. He then created the angels to keep Him company, but that wasn't enough for Him. Next He created the universe and put humans in it. I know that His intentions were to let these humans multiply and then serve Him. I just couldn't take anymore of this worshiping, so I talked to a few of the other angels. Since I was an archangel, I got quite a number of others to go along with my plan to overthrow God and rule the universe ourselves. Well, as you know, there were a few problems. We just didn't have enough time to plan. At least I am the ruler of earth. Everyone has to answer to me here. I tell people what to do, and even when they don't want to . . . they still do what I say.

Night: What about Jesus?

Satan: Jesus showed up one day and told me He was sent by God to take away my kingdom. I tried to get Him to prove it to me. I told Him to show me He was God's Son by doing something simple like turning a rock into bread. He dodged me like a cheap politician. I thought that perhaps He was just some power-hungry kid that wanted people to think He was someone important, so I told Him I would give Him everything I owned if He would just tell me that He wasn't God's Son. He was wise to me though and refused. I even tried to get Him to jump to His death since if He was God's Son, I knew the angels that remained behind with God would have saved Him. Again He refused. Obviously He knew that if He did, He would die. I knew that He was a liar. Then out of revenge He began to preach against me. He scared innocent women and children into believing that if they didn't follow Him they would die and go to a terrible place called hell. He told them I was evil. Well, I got the last laugh, since He died on Calvary.

Night: Thank you. *(Satan leaves.)* Nothing more your honor. The prosecution rests.

Judge: We have heard from the prosecution. There is still no one here to stand in defense of Jesus. Without any evidence to refute what I have heard, I have no alternative but to assume that what I have just heard is the truth. I know it is a little unusual, but this is an unusual case. Is there anyone here in the courtroom that would give some testimony on behalf of this Jesus? Anyone at all? I can only wait a few moments longer . . . Is Jesus really hated this much?

Encourage members in the congregation to stand and give a testimony. Telling a few selected people in advance about what is desired will help bring about a spontaneous movement from others.

AN ANNIVERSARY TO REMEMBER

by Matt Tullos

A humorous look at love in spite of adversity

He: Well, so much for the anniversary date.

She: It was a good idea.

He: Thanks. Sorry some things got kind of —

She: Don't mention it.

He: Really? You're not mad?

She: Me? Nah —

He: Somehow I knew this was going to be one of those nights when I backed out of the garage without opening the garage door. I guess I was just keyed up. I just wanted everything to be right. We haven't had a nice romantic evening in a long time.

She: It's too bad the garage door shattered the rear window of the car when it fell off the hinges but, on the other hand, the night air gave it the feel of a convertible. I liked it.

He: Thanks, Honey. How are your legs?

She: I think they're getting better. I'm beginning to regain feeling in the right one.

He: I had no idea that manhole was uncovered when I opened the door to let you out. It was — now I see you — now I don't!

She: I can't believe the city worker thought that I was intentionally attacking him when I fell on his head in the manhole.

He: I think it must have been the scream. It had a kind of "martial arts" sound to it. I tried to explain the situation to the officer, but he took one look at the car and just said, "Sure, Buddy."

She: At least we got to spend our anniversary together — even if it was in jail. It was nice of your boss to bail us out. How did he know?

He: He said he saw us on the news.

She: We were on the news?

He: At 11 p.m. I had Mom tape it. They thought we were a part of the gang that has been threatening to bomb city hall. It was nice of my boss to pick us up. I hope he wasn't upset about the bad publicity and all.

She: Are you kidding? He wasn't mad. Why he even gave us a card. How sweet. Not many bosses remember their employee's wedding anniversary. Such a nice man.

He: Oh, yeah. That *was* nice of him. I haven't even opened it.

Pulls the card out and opens it.

He: Hmm — I guess he *was* mad after all. He fired me.

She: Look at the bright side of it —

He: What?

She: We have some insurance money for the part of our house that caught fire when the garage door short-circuited the wiring in the garage.

He: The neighbors said their kids really enjoyed seeing the fire trucks. I should have been here to put out the fire.

She: But honey you couldn't be. We were in jail.

He: I know. I know...

She: But look at it this way. Things could be worse.

He: They could?

She: We could be bitter with each other.

He: Yep — we could be heading for divorce court, like the boss and his wife.

She: You could be in love with another woman. We could be so wealthy that we would think more about money than we do about each other.

He: We could be lonely...

She: We could be lost right now, with no faith in Christ.

He: I guess you're right... You're always right.

They kiss.

She: That's because I'm with you. God knew what he was doing when he put us together.

He: *(down about himself)* Yeah — sure.

She: I'm serious. Look, we can still enjoy our night.

He: But we don't have any money. I lost my job — our car — half of our house . . . There's really nothing to enjoy.

She: Sure there is. We have each other. Hey, I have something for you.

She pulls a CD or a cassette from her purse.

He: *The Best of Glen Miller and the Big Band Sound!* I've been looking all over town for this one.

She: I know.

She sticks it in the boom box, they sit close and hold hands, listening to "String of Pearls."

She: I've been saving this for a special occasion.

He: I think this would definitely rate as a special night.

She: I love you.

He: I love you. Happy Anniversary.

She: Happy Anniversary. Let's go to bed and enjoy the stars through our new skylight.

He: Skylight?

She: The fire burned a whole through the ceiling in our bedroom. I've always wanted one of those.

He: You have? Well tomorrow, Sweetheart, I'm going to get a window kit at the hardware store and install a skylight permanently.

She: But we've got to plead "not guilty" of terrorism at the arraignment downtown.

He: Oh yeah, I forgot. *(beat)* Did I hear thunder?

Lights out.

LORD OF MY LIFE

by Randall & Arinée Glass
and J. Scott Reynolds

Who do you worship?

Purpose: *To challenge the audience to love God more than anyone or anything else, and to help them recognize the things we often put before God.*

Adapted from: *Mark 12:30*

Cast:
Off-stage Voice (OSV)
#1: Girl totally infatuated with her boyfriend
#2: Person totally infatuated with self
#3: A video game addict
#4: Football player

Props: *Football, picture of boyfriend, mirror, hand-held video game*

All four characters stand in a line across the stage with their backs to the audience. As each speaks, he turns to the audience and steps forward, returning to his former position when his lines have been spoken.

#1: *(turns around and steps forward holding picture of boyfriend)* Let's pray. Dear Johnny. I am so thankful for you! You are the reason that I live. Johnny—everything I do, I do for you! I live for you, Johnny! When I wake up in the morning, I think of you, Johnny. I am so glad that you chose me to be your girlfriend. Yours always! Amen.

OSV: You must "love the Lord your God with all your heart . . ."

#2: *(steps forward and looks in mirror)* Mirror, mirror in my hand, who is the most handsome in all the land? I am! Praise Me! Let's Pray. Dear ME—I just give you all praise cause I deserve it. I'll give me everything I want. You alone will I serve. No one will get in the way of spending all my money on you and all my time and energy

is for you—ME! Thanks for being such a good-looking, awesome, smart, successful, all around perfect dude! Amen.

OSV: You must "love the Lord your God with all your heart and with all your soul . . ."

#3: Oh, video game you are my shepherd, I shall not want anything but you! You make me to progress through the different levels of difficulty for your name's sake. You lead me beside places where I can find hidden coins and extra men. You even restore my power when I make a mistake. Because of that I won't be afraid. The challenge and the fun you give me comforts me. You prepare the next world for me with plenty of enemies. And I shall dwell in video land forever and ever. Amen

OSV: You must "love the Lord your God with all your heart and with all your soul and with all your mind. . ."

#4: Dear Football! I thank you football for making me the jock that I am. I am devoted to you, football. I always want you with me. All the way 40-30-20-10-5-4-3-2-1 TOUCHDOWN! And we get the glory. My name is in the paper. All the cheerleaders want to go out with me. And money is given to me. With you football, I have purpose and reason. Forever loyal to you, I'll be! Amen.

OSV: You must "love the Lord your God with all your heart and with all your soul and with all your mind and with all your strength." *(Mark 12:30, NIV)*

TEMPTATION

by Christy Doyle

A seeker sketch that reveals the enemy

Cast: *Man, Woman*

Setting: *A restaurant/bar/lounge.* **Woman** *is seated at a table.* **Man** *approaches.*

Props: Lighter, pack of cigarettes, table, chairs

Man: Can I buy you a drink?

Woman: Sorry, I don't drink.

Man: Yeah, neither do I. Mind if I sit down? *(He sits before she has a chance to answer.)*

Woman: *(obviously annoyed)* Yes, I do!

Man: *(pulling out a pack of cigarettes and a lighter)* Would you like a smoke?

Woman: No, thank you. I don't smoke.

Man: Neither do I. *(He puts the cigarettes away and begins to flick the lighter. This continues throughout the scene.)* Has anyone ever told you that you have a *(name of a similar looking celebrity)* look?

Woman: *(laughing)* No, but I have been lied to before.

Man: Well, I'm not lying — but even if I were, what would be wrong with a harmless lie to a beautiful lady?

Woman: Oh, please! Look, I don't mean to be rude, but I'm married — and even if I weren't, you're a little young for me. How old are you, anyway?

Man: How old would you like me to be?

Woman: It doesn't really matter, because I don't care.

Man: Oh, on the contrary. I bet you do care. Say, for example, I was ten years younger than you. I bet you would feel flattered, wouldn't you?

Woman: Yeah, okay. I would. But believe me, I don't go for your type anyway. I never liked the hippie musician-looking kind of guy.

Man: Well, I could probably be any kind of guy you want me to be.

Woman: I don't want you to be "anything." You're making me uncomfortable.

Man: Uncomfortable is good. That means there's an attraction.

Woman: There's no attraction . . . Now, will you leave, please?

Man: I'll do anything for a lady. *(He starts to leave.)* But I'm sure Jim wouldn't mind me talking to his wife.

Woman: Wait! What did you say?

Man: I said, "I'm sure Jim wouldn't mind me talking to his wife."

Woman: How do you know my husband's name?

Man: *(He resumes his seat.)* You'd be surprised at the things I know.

Woman: Like what?

Man: I know you're having marital problems.

Woman: What? — Well, I suppose that's a safe guess. A lot of people have marital problems.

Man: Yes, but I know you cheated on Jim with a coworker for three months.

Woman: What !? Wait a minute! *(confused, thinking)* Oh, I get it! Jim set this up, didn't he? This is some kind of sick joke . . . some kind of test that Jim's set me up for, huh? Who are you? — a friend of Jim's?

Man: I'm everyone's friend — when they least expect it.

Woman: Well, let me make this clear. You're not my friend and I don't like you. *(pause)* Who are you, anyway?

Man: Let's just say my dad is "the father of lies."

Woman: Yeah, well I come from a dysfunctional family, too. But I didn't turn out weird like you.

Man: Flattery will get you everywhere with me.

Woman: I want you to leave.

Man: No, you don't.

Woman: Yes, I do.

Man: Maybe I'm temptation itself.

Woman: No, maybe you're a jerk.

Man: That wouldn't be the worst thing I've been called.

Woman: Who are you anyway?? What do you do for a living?

Man: Have you heard of Beelzebub?

Woman: No, but I'm not up much on all the strange musical groups. So you're a musician, huh? It figures. You look like a musician.

Man: I play on peoples' heartstrings.

Woman: Look if you're not leaving, I am. *(She starts to leave and he grabs her wrist.)* Let go of me or I'll scream. *(He lets go and she rubs her wrist.)* You really burned my arm.

He laughs.

Woman: You are so evil. Here. *(She takes out a gospel tract.)* Someone gave me this Jesus tract today. I think you need it more than I do. *(She starts to walk out, but stops and speaks to herself.)* That guy is scary, but he's . . . well . . . I don't know. There's something that's very attractive about him. *(She exits reluctantly.)*

Man: *(calling after her)* Hey, remember I'm here when you need me, and I'm here even if you don't. *(He sits at the table and examines the tract.)* These are dangerous. We almost lost her. *(He takes the lighter and ignites the tract. He drops it in a large ashtray and watches intently and with great fascination as it burns. If possible the lights should be lowered to underscore the fire's glow on his face. He laughs demonically. Blackout.)*

HERE AM I
by Darrell Cook

What's your excuse?

Cast:
Narrator
Readers #1, #2, #3, #4

Narrator: "Then I heard the voice of the Lord saying, 'Whom shall I send? And who will go for us?' " *(Isa. 6:8, NIV)*

#1: There I was minding my own business and tending sheep, and BOOM — God comes in and tries to turn my life upside down. Lead the people out of Egypt? Who am I that I can be God's spokesman? They won't believe me. They won't even understand me. I've grown up in a palace, they've grown up in slavery. I'm just getting my first taste of work and they've been making bricks and doing construction work for years. They'll never listen to me. I'm not eloquent. I don't speak so good. Now my brother, Aaron, he can talk the ears off a camel. Aaron should lead, not me. *Lord, here am I. Send Aaron!*

Narrator: "Then I heard the voice of the Lord saying, 'Whom shall I send? And who will go for us?' "

#2: Missions? Lord, you can't be calling me to go into missions. I know that every time I hear about mission work I'm moved. And I feel such a burden when I think about the multitudes who have never heard the name of Jesus. But let's face it, I'm not being called to be a mis-

sionary. I like my hometown. I don't want to move far from here. And I like being able to watch television every evening when I get home. Lord, I know they don't show reruns of my favorite shows in Africa. See — it just doesn't make sense for me to be a missionary. But I know who can go, Lord! My sister. She knows a lot about missions because she's never missed a Vacation Bible School. She'd be perfect! *Lord, here am I. Send my sister.*

Narrator: "Then I heard the voice of the Lord saying, 'Whom shall I send? And who will go for us?' "

#3: I feel really sorry for that new neighbor of mine. Having to raise those kids all by herself. It must be tough. Someone really needs to reach out to her. I wish I could help her but I just can't make the time to do it. Between work, my own family, and all the things I do at church, there's just no way. But you know what, Marcie could do it. She lives on our street too, and she's a member of my church. She's got to have time to do it—she doesn't even teach a Sunday School class. It doesn't make sense for me to go see that neighbor. I can't relate to her past as well as Marcie.
Lord, here am I. Send Marcie.

Narrator: "Then I heard the voice of the Lord saying, 'Whom shall I send? And who will go for us?' "

#4: I'm getting nervous, Lord. Joe, my friend at work, found out that I'm a Christian and he keeps asking me questions about my church, about my faith, and about You. I'm in over my head here. I understand the gospel, but I don't know if I could explain it to someone else. I would be too nervous. I studied spiritual gifts in Sunday School and we even took a test to find out what our gifts were. And well . . . I don't remember what my gift was, but I *know* it wasn't evangelism. Lord, could you please send someone to Joe who knows more about the Bible. I know! My pastor can talk to him! He knows about the Bible. *Lord, here am I. Send my pastor.*

Narrator: "Jesus went through all the towns and villages, teaching in their synagogues, preaching the good news of the kingdom and healing every disease and sickness. When he saw the crowds, he had compassion on them, because they were harassed and helpless, like sheep without a shepherd. Then He said to His disciples, 'The harvest is plentiful but the workers are few. Ask the Lord of the harvest, therefore, to send out workers into His harvest field.' " *(Matt. 9:35-38, NIV)*

"Then I heard the voice of the Lord saying, 'Whom shall I send? And who will go for us?' "

And I said . . .

All: Here am I. Send me!

BY OUR LOVE

by Kari L. Todd

Short scenes which challenge teens to love

Cast:
Jessica: Teen daughter of Rachel
Rachel: Mother of Jessica
Matt: Vaughn's younger brother
Vaughn: Matt's teen older brother
Brandi: Teen daughter of parents who aren't home
Rockford: Teen son of Carol
Carol: Mother of Rockford
Narrator

Setting: *Simple staging will work best. Door frame down stage center (to designate a separation of scenes). Stage left has a chair and a small table. Stage right has a chair and a bed.*

SCENE I

Jessica: *(listening to loud earphones, is stage right. Clothes and magazines are thrown about on the floor.)*

Rachel: *(enters through door)* Jessica! Jessica!

Jessica: *(doesn't hear her)*

Rachel: *(walks over to her)* Jessica, I said to turn that thing down!

Jessica: What?! I was just listening to my music.

Rachel: Well, before you do anything else, I want you to clean up this room. It's a PIT! And then I would like you to take out the trash. Those are a part of your chores—remember?

Jessica: *(thinking of an excuse)* Well . . . I can't right now, Mom. I've got to go to Wednesday night Bible study! See Ya! *(she finds her Bible in the mess on the floor and exits quickly)*

Rachel: That's a great attitude, Jessica! Church before your family—they teach you that there? *(to herself)* And she wonders why I don't go to church!

SCENE II

Matt: *(sits stage left, near table)* Oh man!

This just can't be . . . How could this . . . What am I gonna do?

Vaughn: *(enters through door)* Dad! Hey Dad! *(sees Matt)* Oh, it's just you. *(still looking)* Have you seen Dad?

Matt: No, he's not here — out golfing or something. *(takes a beat)* Could I talk to you a minute?

Vaughn: Matt — you always do this! You're always whining about one problem or another. And you know I don't have time to talk. Look, one of my friends at church is having a real hard time so I have to go and see him. *(Punches him on the shoulder)* Good Samaritan, you know!?

Matt: But isn't this the same? — I really need to . . .

Vaughn: *(leaving)* See ya! Tell Dad I'm over at Mike's.

Matt: *(to himself)* "Love your neighbor as yourself . . ." *(Matt.22:39, NIV)* *(louder towards the door)* . . . guess I'd have more luck if I was a neighbor instead of a brother!! *(continuing his thoughts from before)* Man . . . I just don't know what to do . . .

SCENE III

Brandi: *(enters while speaking)* Mom?! Dad? Yo Mom!!! I guess no one is home. *(beat)* Well, I better leave them a note. *(sits at table, writing)*
   "Mom and Dad,
    Gone to church . . .
    Going for pizza after services . . .
    Love . . ."
(looks up) What am I writing them a note for?? They never tell me where they are. And they certainly don't like it when I go to church. They don't care. Forget this! *(Wads up note, tosses it away, then leaves)*

SCENE IV

Carol: *(She is cooking dinner.)* Rock? Rockford!!

Rockford: Mom! Quit your hollerin'!

Carol: Will you please take a look at the car? With your dad gone this week, I don't know what else to do. I heard a weird noise earlier when I came home from the store. Maybe there is something wrong with the thingymabobber . . .

Rockford: Get real Mom. Have a mechanic look at it. *(to himself)* Probably nothing wrong with it anyway.

Carol: We don't have enough money for a mechanic. Now couldn't you just take the time to look at it??

Rockford: *(leaving)* Can't now, Mom. Gotta head over to the church and help them fix the sound system. Can't have the service without it. Just don't drive the car 'til Dad gets back.

Carol: *(upset)* I guess this means you don't want dinner???

SCENE V
*All **Teens** come CS with Bibles in hand, as if at the end of a church service, and mime singing.*

Narator: "This is how God showed His love among us: He sent His one and only Son into the world so that we might live through Him. Dear friends, since God so loved us, we also ought to love one another." *(1 John 4:10, 12, NIV)* By this will all men know that you are my disciples, if you love one another. *(John 13:35, NIV)*

JESUS, ONLY JESUS

by Jeff Atwood

Monologues and choral reading on the uniqueness of Jesus

Cast:
Mary Magdalene
Thaddeus
Woman at the Well
Blind Man

Does not need to be done in biblical costume.

Mary Magdalene: We had brought a basket of spices to anoint His body. As we were walking down the dusty path to the graveyard, we realized that the huge stone the Romans had placed in front of the opening to this borrowed grave would be in place. The guards would never think of moving the stone to let us in. We rounded the corner to get to the place where they had laid Him, and we saw it. Actually , we saw the opening to the grave and *not* the stone, for it had been rolled away. Could someone have stolen Jesus' body? Did the Romans move Him as some sort of final insult? All that was in the tomb was a pile of linen cloth and the burial clothes. Later, after the others had come to see the empty tomb and then left, I was there alone. I heard a familiar voice call my name, "Mary." It was my Lord! He was alive! He had moved the stone that we could never move. We had gotten to the tomb not knowing what we could do to move the stone, but once again, like He had done a thousand times before, He did for me what I could not do for myself. It was Jesus, only Jesus . . .

Overlapping on "only Jesus"

Thaddeus: . . . Only Jesus could sleep through this kind of storm. It had come out of nowhere. Even Peter and Andrew, James and John, the fishermen who had faced every kind of storm, were frightened. The wind had whipped the waves into a fury. The boat was shaking, and we were sure we would be lost over the side. I went to the back of the boat and woke Jesus. He arose and spoke to the wind and waves, "Peace. Be still." And as quickly as the storm had come, the sea became soft, and calm, and gentle. It was the same way for me. Many times over, it was not the sea that He would calm, it was my own fears. Fears about life, about death. He was the only one who could change the weather with a word. And he was the only one who could mend a heart and save a life with the same words. "Peace. Be still." The one who can do that is Jesus, only Jesus . . .

Overlapping on "only Jesus"

Woman at the Well: . . . Only Jesus had the words of life. All that I had was a past. I went to the well at noon to avoid those who made a point to shame me. He asked me how I was. But not like the others who were asking for selfish reasons. He had come to the well, not to quench *His* thirst, but to quench *my* thirst. Jesus came where I *was*, so that I might be where He *was going*. He made a way for me to Him because there was no way I could get there on my own. I was a woman with a past. He was the Savior who gave me a future. The one way I could get beyond myself was Jesus, only Jesus . . .

Overlapping on "only Jesus"

Blind Man: . . . Only Jesus stopped when I called out, asking for help. I had been born blind. Jesus stepped away from the crowd of people that surrounded Him, and He walked over to me, and healed me. He opened my eyes to see the things I could not see, and He opened my heart to know the things I had never known. He let me see the world. But more importantly, He let me see love. Jesus, only Jesus . . .

At each point where the different actors speak "Jesus, only Jesus," they should overlap and speak in unison, so the whole piece is a continuous train of thought and sound.

Mary: . . . Jesus, only Jesus does the things that I cannot. Jesus, only Jesus . . .

Thaddeus: . . . Jesus, only Jesus could calm the raging in my soul. Jesus, only Jesus . . .

Woman: . . . Jesus, only Jesus could share the blessed words of life. Jesus, only Jesus . . .

Blind Man: . . . Jesus, only Jesus could let me see true love. Jesus, only Jesus . . .

Mary: . . . Jesus, only Jesus could split all time in two. Jesus, only Jesus . . .

Thaddeus: . . . Jesus, only Jesus could rescue me and you. Jesus, only Jesus . . .

Woman: . . . Jesus, only Jesus could be the final sacrifice. Jesus, only Jesus . . .

Blind Man: . . . Jesus, only Jesus could offer grace, and peace, and life. Jesus, only Jesus . . .

Slowing down with emphasis

All: . . . Jesus, only Jesus.

ETERNALLY GRATEFUL

by Christy Doyle

A great sketch that merges Thanksgiving and evangelism

Cast: *Charles* and *James*

Setting: *A train station.*

Charles, stands downstage "outside" of the scene as he addresses the audience.

Charles: I'd like to tell you about a special Thanksgiving story that happened ten years ago.

He walks into the scene carrying a small suitcase and is obviously waiting for someone. James enters and approaches him.

James: Excuse me, sir. May I ask you a question?

Charles: Sure, but make it fast. My future in-laws should be here any minute to pick me up. Only I would be crazy enough to pick Thanksgiving weekend to get married.

James: Do you know Jesus Christ?

Charles: Do I look that old, buddy? He died. Didn't you hear? It was about two thousand years ago.

James: Yes, He did die — for me and you, and He rose again.

Charles: Yeah, and I bet he moved in with you, right? Maybe you'd better run back home and let him out of the basement — invite him to Thanksgiving dinner.

James: I'd like to show you some scriptures.

Charles: Yeah, and I'd like to show you that revolving door. Where's a good security guard when you need one?

James: What's your name, sir?

Charles: Well, it isn't "stupid," buddy, so will you go find someone else to bother?

James: I'd like to know your name, sir.

Charles: If I tell you my name will you leave me alone?

James: No.

Charles: Great. This is all I need. Debbie's parents are going to think you're a friend of mine.

James: I'd like to be your brother.

Charles: I don't have a brother, alright? And believe me, I don't need any.

James: Well, brother, I'd like to pray for you.

Charles: Good! Pray yourself away, will you? And please don't call me "brother."

James: Well, brother, if I knew your name I could do just that.

Charles: It's Charles, OK?—It's Charles, Chuck, or Charlie—but don't call be "brother," ok?

James: Ok, Charles, my name is James. I'm going to put you on my prayer list.

Charles: Great. I'm on every other junk mailing list. Could you go bother some other "brother" now?

James: Have you been born again?

Charles: No, but I'd like to be born again in another time zone.

James: Do you know Jesus as your personal Savior?

Charles: Are you for real?

James: I met Jesus on a train.

Charles: Oh, he must not have been on my connection from New York City— but Elvis was. We had peanut butter and banana sandwiches in the dining car.

James: I don't mean I met Him literally.

Charles: Did you just say something that made sense?

James: Perfect sense. I met someone who told me about Jesus.

Charles: Look, did anybody ever tell you that you talk about Jesus in a church, not in a train station?

James: Those who seek God find Him — no matter where they're looking.

Charles: Well, I'm not looking for God. I'm looking for my future in-laws. They must be lost.

James: So are you, Charles

Charles: I'm not lost. I'm in a train station.

James: You're lost in God's eyes.

Charles: Oh, really? Well then I guess God isn't so powerful if He can't find me.

James: He will. He loves you more than you can comprehend. Do you know you're a sinner?

Charles: Yeah, but let's just keep that our little secret, shall we?

James: Did you know that Jesus died for your sins?

Charles: Well, he could have saved himself a lot of trouble because I'm not exactly grateful.

James: John 3:16 says, "For God so loved the world, that He gave His only begotten Son, that whosoever believeth in him should not perish, but have everlasting life." *(KJV)* You must believe in Him.

Charles: No, I need to believe that you will eventually disappear.

James: You will too, someday, and where will you go?

Charles: I don't know, because I won't be here! Look, Jim —

James: James.

Charles: James. I've had a long train ride and I'm going to stuff myself with turkey for two days and then get married. I'm under a lot of stress. I'd just like some peace.

James: Jesus can give you that peace.

Charles: You have an answer for everything, don't you?

James: No, but Jesus does. You need to talk with Him.

Charles: No, I need to talk with my in-laws. I gotta go make a phone call.

James: Here, take this literature. *(He hands him some tracts.)*

Charles exits out of the scene and observes. James is forlorn.

James: I did it again didn't I, Lord? I pushed too hard. That guy thinks I'm a religious kook—I know he does. I don't know how to do this thing right. I don't know what made me talk to that guy. I just felt I should. I guess I can't go wrong telling people about You — at least I hope not. I'm sorry I messed up, Lord. Oh, well, it's not like I'm ever going to see the guy again. *(He exits.)*

Charles: But he will see me again. *(He pulls a small Bible out of his pocket.)* Five years ago they put a "Reverend" in front of my name. So you see, Thanksgiving will always be special to me. That year *(He gestures toward the train station scene.)* I got my wife, and the next year I got eternal life! And every year, I'm eternally grateful to James. *(He starts to exit, but pauses.)* The poor guy probably still thinks he failed that day. Boy, is he going to be surprised. *(He exits.)*

THE LIFEBOAT

by Claire Hamilton

A parable of attitudes about saving the lost

Cast: *Person 1 (female); Person 2 (male)*

Setting: *A rubber lifeboat in the ocean*

Props: *Binoculars*

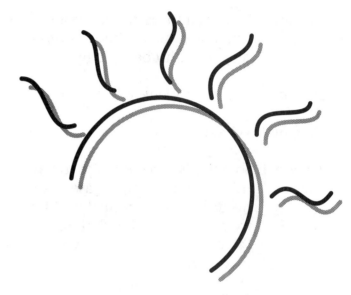

Person 1: *(looking out across the sea with binoculars)* We've been drifting for what seems like years.

Person 2: Oh, just sit back and enjoy the sun!

Person 1: If I enjoy the sun much longer, I'm going to be sunburned. *(looks at arms)*

Person 2: You're always looking for a reason to rock the boat. *(mimics **Person 1**)* The food is old. The water is salty. The boat's too small. We can't expand it any larger. Just learn to go with the flow.

Person 1: I can't help it if I have an eye for improvement.

Person 2: Improvement! Try discontentment! Things are just fine. We're drifting along . . . no winds . . . no rough waves. Nice and easy.

Person 1: Okay, Okay. *(looks out to sea)* Hey! Somebody's out there. We've got to help them. *(begins to yell)* Hey! We're over here. Swim this way!

Person 2: Are you crazy! Let me see that. *(looks through binoculars)* Oh my, did you see the way he swims? He throws his arms and stirs up the water. We can't have him in here . . . he'll rock the boat.

Person 1: But the waves are so rough!

Person 2: And whose fault is that? Don't worry, a cruise ship will pick him up. He would feel more comfortable on a cruise ship than in our little boat.

Person 1: But he looks as if he's sinking.

Person 2: Well, if he would just tread water, he wouldn't sink, would he?

Person 1: I guess not. *(looks again)* There's another person. She looks in trouble.

Person 2: Well, let me see. *(takes binoculars)* Oh, did you see the way she's dressed? We can't have her in here. What will the Coast Guard say when they pick us up if she's with us?

Person 1: But there are sharks out there! We've got to do something! She'll drown out there.

Person 2: You need to learn that we are a small boat, we can't save everyone. We must be selective.

Person 1: But what about us?

Person 2: What about us?

Person 1: Somebody cared enough to have this lifeboat ready, in case it was needed, and we needed it. When we reached out that dark night in the cold rough waves, it was there. There to save us.

Person 2: Well, that's different. We're not like those people. Everyone has his place and this is not it.

Person 1: *(sighs, begins to look out again with binoculars)* I don't believe it.

Person 2: Now what?

Person 1: It can't be. It's impossible.

Person 2: What? *(grabs binoculars and looks . . . then slowly lowers them)*

Person 1: Did you see it?

Person 2: *(nods slowly)* It's incredible . . . somebody's out there, all right.

Person 1: Yeah . . . and he's walking on the water. It's our Captain! What are we going to do?

Person 2: Clean up this mess. We can't have Him seeing all this garbage.

Person 1: We're fine! Believe me. We have kept afloat. We haven't made any waves. We go through the survival guide once a week. He might even give us a medal!

Person 2: You're right. Straighten your tie. Good Morning Captain! Fine day to drift, isn't it?

Person 2: *(looks in binoculars, lowers them)*

Person 1: What is it? What's wrong?

Person 2: He's headed in the other direction!

THE 23RD PSALM

by James F. DeLong

A creative interpretation of scripture that could also be a responsive reading

Adapted from: Psalm 23 *(KJV)*
Cast: *#1* and *#2*
Setting: *Characters stand on opposite sides of the stage.*

#1: The Lord is my Shepherd;

#2: I am His sheep. I would go astray without His guidance, His care, His love.

#1: I shall not want.

#2: He gives me everything I need, not necessarily what I want.

#1: He maketh me to lie down in green pastures:

#2: I get caught up in today's fast-paced world, and He slows me down, has me "stop and smell the roses," for my own good.

#1: He leadeth me beside the still waters.

#2: He takes me to the quiet places, where I can rest, think, and renew myself.

#1: He restoreth my soul:

#2: When I am broken, He puts me back together.

#1: He leadeth me in the paths of righteousness for His name's sake.

#2: He does this for His glory, for I am unworthy.

#1: Yea, though I walk through the valley of the shadow of death,

#2: We all die. Loved ones go on before us, and then it's our turn.

#1: I will fear no evil: for thou art with me: thy rod and thy staff they comfort me.

#2: He has passed through death's door and has returned to bring me safely through to the other side.

#1: Thou preparest a table before me in the presence of mine enemies;

#2: He will make me triumphant, having suffered for His name.

#1: Thou anointest my head with oil; my cup runneth over.

#2: He will honor me. He will bless me far beyond my expectations or imagination.

#1: Surely goodness and mercy shall follow me all the days of my life: and I will dwell in the house of the Lord forever.

#2: Through His grace, I will share Heaven with Him, my family, and my friends, forever.

Both: Amen.

COME LET US REASON

by Matt Tullos

Adapted from: *Isaiah 1:18 & 55:6-7*

Cast: *Readers #1, #2, #3,* and *#4*

#1: What does sin smell like?

#2: Smoke

#3: Spoiled stench of garbage

#4: Three days of sweat

#1: Layers of old, unkempt clothes

#3: The burning flesh of the DMZ

All: Auschwitz

#2 & #3: South Central LA

#1 & #4: Homeless bums

#2: Serbian rebels

#3: Cheap perfume

#4: on 16th avenue.

#1: 200 dollar champagne and caviar

#2: in close proximity to a freezing mother

#4: Clinging to a new born baby

#3: outside a shelter where there is no home.

All: Or could it be

#1: Could it smell like

#2: Fresh cut flowers

#3: New carpet

#4: Facilities built in the name of One who does not dwell in buildings.

#1: Could sin smell like an exclusive feast on Wednesday night?

#2: Could it smell like boardrooms, offices, and diplomas?

#1: Church members too intoxicated with pride to see

#2: the lost,

#3: the dying,

#4: the hopeless.

#2: Those seeking to know what we are too busy to tell.

#3: Blind guides

#4: Dry bones

#1: Older Brothers

#2: Wicked and unjust servants

#3: You

#4: Me

All: All of us...

#4: Where are we going?

#1: What is that smell?

#2: Could it be—

All: The Bride of Christ?

#3: "Let us seek the Lord while He may be found,

#1: Call upon Him while He is near.

#4: Let the wicked forsake his way and the unrighteous man his thoughts;

#2: Let him return to the Lord,
And He will have mercy on him,

#1: And to our God, For He will freely pardon." *(Isa. 55:6-7, NKJV)*

#2: "Come now, and let us reason together,

#3: Says the Lord.

#4: Though your sins are like scarlet,

#2: They shall be as white as snow;

#3: Though they are red as crimson,

#1: They shall be as wool." *(Isa. 1:18, NKJV)*

#1 & #2: Come let us reason.

#3 & #4: Come let us reason.

All: Come...

TIME WITH GOD

by Tammy Toney

This piece fits well within the standard worship setting

Cast: **Woman** and **God** (voice only)

Scene: **Choir** enters for the morning worship service. The **choir** sits down. The organ or piano continues to play softly. One **Female Choir Member** stands as if to leave, and then begins to act out what she is thinking.

Woman: *(in frustration)* I can't. I can't do it anymore. Who am I trying to kid! I am not fit to be up here today. Why am I here? I know why I'm here, but I'm just not ready to be here. Look at me, I'm supposed to be a worship leader — what a joke. How can I be a leader of any kind when everything I try to do turns out wrong? Well, not everything, but it seems like everything.

God: What's wrong?

Woman: *(looking up and around)* What's wrong? Come on God, I don't expect to have to explain to *You* what's wrong. Didn't you hear me in that Sunday School class? I made a total fool of myself. All the preparing I did and I still went in there and sounded like I'd never seen the lesson before. And Lord, You know those kids better than I do, and we both know that whether they admit it or not, they think I'm stupid.

God: Stupid! Where do you suppose that came from?

Woman: And they're right God, I do feel so stupid. It wasn't necessarily a simple lesson, but, good grief, I've been in church all of my life, and I should at least be able to teach a kids' Sunday School class.

God: You did teach Sunday School and I'm grateful for your commitment and your faithfulness.

Woman: How can You thank *me*? I did a terrible job. Nothing came out like I planned it. Those kids won't remember a word I said. I don't think they even understood what the Scriptures meant.

God: You gave them the Scriptures, I'll give them understanding. You did your job, I'll do Mine.

Woman: And God, not only did I mess up the lesson, but I let myself get distracted and angry at the kids. I don't like getting upset with them. I just want them to learn. I know that I can't control *their* actions but I should be able to control my *own*.

God: It's okay, we all get angry at some point, but the important thing is that you don't stay there. Anger can be very defeating and can eventually destroy you if you let it.

Woman: But it's *not* okay. *I'm* not okay! It's not just what happened in class today, it's just that there is always something. Something or somebody always discourages me or makes me feel inadequate and defeated. And now, I'm supposed to come to worship. No, wait a minute, I'm supposed to be a worship leader. Do I look like I'm in any shape to be a worship leader? Do I look like I'm in any shape to worship? To praise?

God: Look at Me. I'll help you. But you have to look at *Me*.

Woman: *(looking down)* I can't. Why do I bother? I shouldn't have come today. I'm not sure why I'm here anyway.

God: You're here because I brought you here.

Woman: You brought me here. Surely You don't enjoy seeing me in the shape I'm in. If this is what You're after, then I hope You're satisfied.

God: I brought you here today because this is exactly where you need to be, and because I love you.

Woman: You love me. I've read that all of my life. The Bible is full of examples of how You love me, but I have to be honest with You, You certainly have a strange way of showing it.

God: Your experiences this morning haven't been pleasant, I know that, but it is because of them that you have turned to Me. I brought you here because I love you and because I want to spend time with you.

Woman: I wanted to spend time with You too, but that was before I became so frustrated and discouraged, and now I'm in no position to be with you, and certainly not to *look* at You.

God: What position do you need to be in?

Woman: I mean, it's been a crazy morning. My attitude is not exactly wonderful. If my heart is not acceptable to me, it certainly cannot be acceptable to You. I shouldn't even be in this worship service. I want to serve You, God. I long to be with You, but days like this make it so hard. I *think* my heart is right, but when I'm so easily defeated I really start to wonder.

God: You just keep your eyes and your heart *focused on Me* and I promise you will experience worship. And when you worship Me nothing else will matter.

Woman: But what about this morning?

God: Don't worry about this morning. The only thing that matters right now is that you focus on Me.

Woman: But my attitude is so . . .

God: Look this way.

Woman: I . . .

God: Please, please look at Me.

Choir sings, a cappella, the chorus to "Turn Your Eyes Upon Jesus." [1] *Lights fade, spotlight is left on woman who slowly lifts her head and eyes toward heaven. As the choir finishes, she says quietly:*

Woman: Thank you, Lord. *(She sits.)*

---

[1] *The Baptist Hymnal*, 1991, No. 320.

SET FREE

by Christal Hughes

Cast: *Biblical Character, 1800's Character, Modern Day Character, and Narrator*

Costumes: *One biblical outfit, one 1800's outfit, one present day outfit*

Narrator: *(walks on stage)* "Jesus Christ is the same yesterday and today and forever." (Heb. 13:8, NIV)

Biblical Character: *(Enters and begins to tell of meeting Jesus.)* They said He — this man Jesus — was different. Said that when He was near, it was as though time stood still. I really couldn't understand. Then it happened. I was walking outside of town that day and saw a large crowd on a hill. As I approached, I heard His voice — it was like no other I had ever heard. It was as if the words He spoke were just for me. They reached into my soul and began to chip away at all the sin I had carried for years. I had never felt such love. No matter what I had done — I was forgiven. As I let go of myself and my past, I gave my all to Him — I was set free.

Narrator: *(Walks on stage.)* "Jesus Christ is the same yesterday and today and forever."

1800's Character: *(Enters and begins to tell of meeting Jesus.)* My family had always gone into town on Sunday morning to church. You see we lived on a farm about two miles out. I had heard of Jesus since I'd been little, but still felt unsure. Then it happened, Pa left his Bible on the table that morning, so I said I'd run back and get it. I went to grab for it off the table and it fell open to the book called John. As I picked it up and my eyes fell on the words on the page, I heard His voice. It was like no other I had ever heard. It was as if the words He spoke were just for me. They reached into my soul and began to chip away at the sin I had carried for years. I had never felt such love. No matter what I had done — I was forgiven. As I let go of myself and my past, I gave my all to Him — I was set free.

Narrator: *(Walks on stage.)* "Jesus Christ is the same yesterday and today and forever."

Modern Day Character: *(Enters and begins to tell of meeting Jesus.)* I couldn't stand it anymore. Nothing was right. My family was at each other's throats all the time. School was getting harder. I had started doing things — parties, relationships, things I knew I shouldn't — but it just didn't seem to matter. Then It happened. A girl I knew from school asked me to go to the game with her Friday night. There was something about her — something different. She came over to my house after the game. We started talking, she said she had found something she wanted me to have. She took out a little Bible and showed me this story about God's Son. I heard His voice. It was like no other I had ever heard. It was as if the words He spoke were just for me. They reached into my soul and began to chip away at all the sin I had carried for years. I had never felt such love. No matter what I had done — I was forgiven. As I let go of myself and my past, I gave my all to Him — I was set free.

PARABLE OF THE SOILS

by Matt and Shea Williams

Visualizing the parable through mime

Adapted from: *Matthew 13:1-9,18-23*

Cast: *Clowns or Mimes (14 or more): 1 narrator, 1 farmer, 4 "seeds," 1 snatcher, 2 mockers, 3 "symbols" representing the "cares of this world," extra seeds*

Props: *Bible for narrator*

12 small Bibles

12 construction paper hearts

*3 boxes (for three **symbols** to hold)*

1) "job" (in box: toy phone, files, datebook, etc.)

2) "$" (in box: toy car, play money, etc.)

3) "fun" (in box: toy boat, football, etc.)

Narrator *reads Matthew 13:1-9 as other clowns or mimes demonstrate Jesus' explanation in Matthew 13:18-23. **Narrator** should not read scripture <u>references</u> aloud.*

Narrator: "That same day Jesus went out of the house and sat by the lake. Such large crowds gathered around him that he got into a boat and sat in it, while all the people stood on the shore. Then he told them many things in parables, saying: 'A farmer went out to sow his seed.' *(vv. 1-3)*

*The **4 Main Seeds** are on their knees, hunched over. The **Farmer** comes out and acts as if scattering seeds. He hands the **4 Seeds** each a Bible. Each is wearing a heart already. Then farmer exits.*

Narrator: 'As he was scattering the seed, some fell along the path, and the birds came and ate it up.' *(v. 4)*

*The **First Seed** pops up partially, but the **Snatcher** comes in quickly and snatches the* seed's heart and Bible. The **Seed** drops dead. The **Snatcher** laughs and then exits.

Narrator: 'Some fell on rocky places, where it did not have much soil. It sprang up quickly, because the soil was shallow. But when the sun came up, the plants were scorched, and they withered because they had no root.' *(v. 5-6)*

The **Second Seed** pops up all the way quickly and acts real excited. Then two **Mockers** come by and mime laughing at him. So, he looks at his Bible and throws it and his heart down. Then he drops dead.

Narrator: 'Other seed fell among thorns, which grew up and choked the plants.' *(v. 7)*

The **Third Seed** grows up casually. The **Three Symbols** representing the "cares of this world" come in giving seed various things. He is holding his Bible in his left hand. He holds other things in right hand until the last symbol. He needs to use his left hand to hold symbol. He looks at his Bible, then at symbol, back at Bible. He decides to put down the Bible to hold the symbol. Then he holds the symbol and falls over dead.

Narrator: 'Still other seed fell on good soil, where it produced a crop — a hundred, sixty, or thirty times what was sown.' (v. 8)

The **fourth seed** grows casually, stretches, looks at heaven and Bible. **Extra seeds** are hunched over behind **main seeds**.

After the **Fourth Seed** becomes a "plant," he distributes hearts and Bibles to **Extra Seeds**. The **First 3 Seeds** stay dead. **Extra Seeds** grow up and stretch hands to heaven.

After **Fourth Seed** is back in place and **all Plants** are reaching up to heaven, **Narrator** reads verse 9.

Narrator: 'He who has ears, let him hear.' " (v.9)

All scriptures are from the *NIV* version.

LOST AND FOUND

by Al Hunter

Finding your way on the Roman Road

Cast: *Clerk, Honest, Backslider, Lost* *All roles may be either male or female. Use appropriate gender titles and pronouns throughout.*

*Scene opens with **Clerk** behind desk, as other three actors line up to be served.*

C: Thank you very much, Mr. Honest. I'm sure whoever lost this purse will be forever grateful for your turning it in.

H: Oh, I wouldn't think of doing anything else with it.

C: Have a nice day.

H: You, too. *(leaves)*

C: Next? *(**B** moves to desk while **L** stays in place looking aimlessly around.)* And how may I help you, Mr. . . . ?

B: Backslider's the name, thank you. I'm here looking for a Bible. Well, not just any Bible, my personal Bible.

C: Could you describe it? *(picks up pen)*

B: Oh, sure. My mother gave it to me when I was a child. It's black, about this thick *(indicates with thumb & forefinger)* and has the name "Holy Bible" on its front.

C: Yes, I see *(a little coolly)*. And when did you discover it was missing?

B: Just last week when I got ready to go to church.

C: All right. Now, when was the last time you saw it . . . and where?

B: The last time I was at church . . . at church.

C: Could you be a little more precise, with a date, maybe?

B: Well, I guess it was about mumble, mmm

C: *(cupping ear with hand)* I beg your pardon?

B: *(sheepishly)* About seven years ago.

C: Well, Mr. Backslider, I'm fairly certain we haven't had your Bible turned in here. Why don't you just go back to the church? I'm sure they'll do their best to help you locate your Bible, or another.

B: But I'd be embarrassed to show up without it.

C: Don't be. It's more embarrassing not to show up at all.

B: I guess. Thank you very much. *(leaves)*

C: You're welcome. Have a nice day. Next?

L still just shuffles in place, gazing.

C: *(more insistent)* May I help you, Sir?

L: Oh, uh . . . oh, I surely hope so.

C: And *how* may I help you?

L: This is the Lost and Found?

33

C: Yes, it is.

L: And is it for the Lost *or* Found?

C: *(a little annoyed)* Yes, Sir, it is.

L: Well, I think I'm lost.

C: *(aside)* Is that a name or an understatement? *(back to Lost)* And is that lost as in misplaced, or forgotten?

L: Yes.

C: *(pause)* Well, which one?

L: One or the other. I may be in the wrong place, and nobody has come to tell me how to get to the right place, so I must be forgotten.

C: I see. So where do you think you are?

L: Right here. At the Lost and Found.

C: That's for sure. And where do you want to go?

L: To the Right Place.

C: Okay. I'm sure you can get there if you take the Roman Road.

L: *(takes out pad and pencil to make notes)* Take the Roman Road. Okay.

C: Since all have sinned and come short of God's plan and purpose for us, turn right at 3:23.

L: *(writing)* Turn right at 323.

C: Yes. Now at 6:23 you'll find that the payment for our sin is death.

L: I don't know how much I've earned, but I'll stop there anyway.

C: No, don't stop there; turn back to 5:8 because God shows His love to us in that while we were still in sin, Christ died for us.

L: Hmmm. Back to fifty-eight to see that I don't get paid as a sinner because this person died.

C: That's five eight. You see, if you recognize your imperfections and confess them to God with your mouth, and believe in your heart that God raised Jesus from the dead, it says at 10:9 that you will be saved.

L: Ten nine; let's see, that's one-oh-nine and you say the grave is empty?

C: Yes. Finally, at 10:13 you'll find that everyone who follows this road and calls on the name of the Lord shall be saved.

L: *(brightens up)* Okay! Go on to one-oh-one-three and call on the Lord.

C: And you'll find you're on your way to the Right Place.

L: Great! Now let me read this back to see if I have it right. I get on Roman Road by turning right at 323 because everybody usually turns wrong, then I go on to the bank at 623 where I find out that I don't get paid if I turn back to this graveyard at 58 where Christ died because of love; but if I go on to 109 I'll be convinced that the grave is empty. So then I go all the way to 1019 and call for the Lord and He'll show me how to get to the Right Place.

C: That's it.

L: Boy, this Roman Road is a long street with lots of turns.

C: Oh, no. It's straight and narrow.

L: *(shakes head as he turns slowly towards audience and looks up)* Lord, I know I'm lost, and I'm convinced now that nothing I do will change that. My only hope is that this Christ who is dying for my love will set me straight. So, that settles it, I'll get on the Roman Road and follow Him!

PEOPLE NEED THE LORD

by Leigh Ann Thomas

Waking up to the emotions around you...

Cast: *Three Women*

Note: This sketch is more effective with a soft instrumental background. Three microphones are placed side by side. Characters stand with backs to audience until time for them to speak. Each character turns around slowly, speaks, then turns back around.

Woman 1: My name is DESPAIR. I don't know what else could possibly go wrong in my life. I've lost my job and my family. No one cares about me, why should I care about myself?

Woman 2: Hey . . . what are you looking at!? You know, you church people make me sick with all your fine clothes and fine automobiles. I've had it! I don't need you, I don't need anything! Yeah, my name is ATTITUDE, you got a problem with that?

Woman 3: My name is LONELINESS. I have everything . . . a family, friends, a good job, a nice home. But something just seems to be missing. There's a void in my life that I just can't seem to fill.

Woman 1: There's nothing I can't accomplish on my own. If there's something I want, you'd better not get in my way. Look out for number one, right? My name is SELF.

Woman 2: I stay at home with my children and sometimes I think I'm going to lose my mind. I want to be a good mother, but it seems like I'm always screaming at the kids! I can't seem to be what the world says I should be . . . perfect wife, perfect mother . . . career woman. My name is FRUSTRATION.

Woman 3: The group I hang out with is having a demonstration next week. You know, against those people who don't belong here. Our race is the only one God approves of, you know. The others have to go. My name is HATE.

Woman 1: I don't see what the big deal is about life. It's just one long monotonous ordeal to me. Who cares about anything? I certainly don't. My name is APATHY.

Woman 2: My family is in a cycle that we just can't seem to get out of. We barely have food on the table and clothes for the children. I don't know what to do or where to turn. My name is POVERTY.

Woman 3: You all should see my new car. It's the ultimate in transportation. And I bet you just wish you could take a look in my closet, the best clothes money can buy! And I'm going shopping again tomorrow. Actually I could shop 24 hours a day! It's my life. My name is POSSESSIONS.

Woman 1: I've been so depressed lately. I just can't seem to shake it. I wish I had just one good friend . . . someone to talk to. I've seen you around. You and your family are always doing things together and you seem so happy. I wish you'd share your secret with me. I am your NEIGHBOR.

Woman 2: I am a MEMBER of _____ church. A quite important member, if you ask me. You won't catch *me* sitting down. I'm *always* busy working for the church. This personal relationship with the Lord stuff gets on my nerves a little though. Who needs it? As long as I'm working hard, that's enough . . . isn't it?

Woman 3: You know, just because *you* have it all together doesn't mean I do. I've been watching you go to church for years, but you've never actually looked into my eyes and talked with me about this Jesus stuff. I *really* need you to do that. I am your WIFE. (*stays facing audience*)

Woman 2: I am your SON. (*stays facing audience*)

Woman 1: I am your DAUGHTER.

All slowly turn back around together.

JESUS LOVES ME!
by Neal Breeding

A great addition to a children's worship time!

The song "Jesus Loves Me" (by Anna B. Warner) is sung one time through. Then each line is sung, with interruptions.

#1: *(singing)* "Jesus"

#2: *(speaking)* Hey, we're talking about Jesus. You know. The Son of God; who became human like you and me and lived a sinless life while he was on this earth.

#1: "loves me!"

#2: He not only loves us. But He loves you and you and you and you, but not just you and you and you— but He loves all of your friends, your family, your enemies — I mean — everyone!

#1: "This I know,"

#2: I know this for a fact. Not just up here in my head, but down here in my heart where I will never forget.

#1: "For the Bible tells me so."

#2: It really does! It tells me in John 3:16 that God loved the world, (that's us!) ...and He gave His one and only Son... (that's Jesus!)... if anyone believes in Him... and asks Him to be Lord...will not die... (which is separation from God in Hell)... but have eternal life... (which is living with Jesus forever in heaven). Really, that's what it says! If you don't believe me, look it up for yourself!

#1: "Little ones to Him belong;"

#2: Now we're not just talking about babies, because we all start out that way. But if we ask Jesus to be our Lord, we again become spiritual babies. With a new start! Spiritual babies that now belong to Him.

#1: "They are weak, but He is strong."

#2: Although we are weak when we become followers of Jesus. He is strong. I mean stronger than all the super heroes on TV combined! And that's pretty strong. And it is through His strength that we become stronger.

#1: "Yes, Jesus loves me!"

#2: And you and you and you... (pointing to different members of the audience)

#1: "Yes, Jesus loves me. Yes, Jesus loves me. The Bible tells me so."

#1 & #2: Why don't you sing it with us to Him!

As the audience begins to sing, players exit.

GONE FISHING

by Annie Ruth Yelton

Great introduction to the apostle John

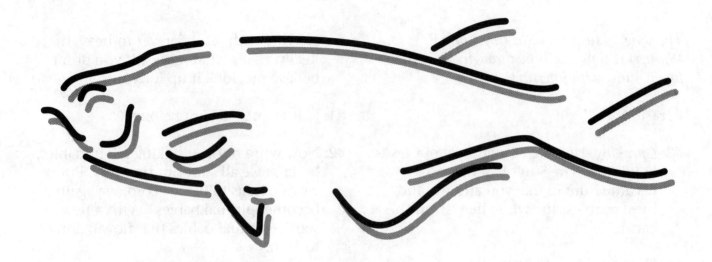

Cast: *Jesus*, apostles *James* and *John*

James and *John* enter from stage right already deep in discussion. *James* drags a piece of fishing net.

James: But John, we must have the new net before we go out again. This old one is torn badly and ragged. *(He holds net toward John.)*

John: *(impatiently)* Yes, yes, I know, but Father wants to go fishing very early in the morning and Josiah says the new one will not be ready before noon tomorrow.

James: *(sulkily)* That is because he rises too late in the day to begin his work.

John: Perhaps, but remember, he is an old man and his step is slow.

Jesus enters from stage right, unnoticed by the two men.

James: Yes-s-s *(impatiently)*, but can we not use that one of Simon and Andrew hanging by?

John: *(The two men glance at **Jesus** as He approaches, but pay Him no attention.)* No, James, the one hanging on their boat has a large tear too, right in the middle.

Jesus: Young men, come and follow me. *(He motions with His hand to come.)*

James: *(Both James and John look toward Jesus as he walks over to them.)* Who, me?

John: You mean us?

Jesus: Yes, come, follow Me and I will make you to become fishers of men.

John: Where are we going?

James: Where do you live?

Jesus: Come with Me, and see. *(He motions with His hand to come.)*

All three men turn as if to leave. **Jesus** *and* **James** *exit.* **James** *scoops up the net and carries it with him.* **John** *remains on stage as the lights dim briefly to indicate the passage of time.*

John: *(lights up again)* For three years we walked the dusty roads of Galilee by Jesus' side. We heard Him teach the multitudes, the many, *many* people who thronged to hear Him, to have Him heal their sick, the blind, the lame. His words were so different from the nit-picking rules of the scribes and Pharisees. He spoke with authority and yet with compassion. Even little children were drawn to Him. *(pause, as if remembering)* I remember the time He fed all of us with one little boy's lunch . . . and we disciples were worried about *pennies*

to buy enough bread! Oh, how small our faith was at times! How patiently He tried to teach us that the kingdom of God was not earthly, but spiritual. When He was crucified, we thought that all was lost. Indeed, life seemed as black as the sky that midday as I stood at the foot of the cross with Mary and heard Him breathe His final breath. *(Facial expression and body language change from doom to joy.)*

Finished. Yes, salvation's plan was finished, but we had just begun to be fishers of men! Before He left us, He commissioned us to share His good news with everyone in Jerusalem, in Judea, in Samaria, and to the ends of the earth.

Many years have passed since the day Jesus called my brother and me. He has been with us, just as He promised He would be. His power and peace have been ours as we preached and healed in His name.

Now I live in a cave on the Isle of Patmos, banished here by the emperor. I do not know what work my Lord has for me here, but I am sure He will continue to be with me and I shall serve Him as long as I live.

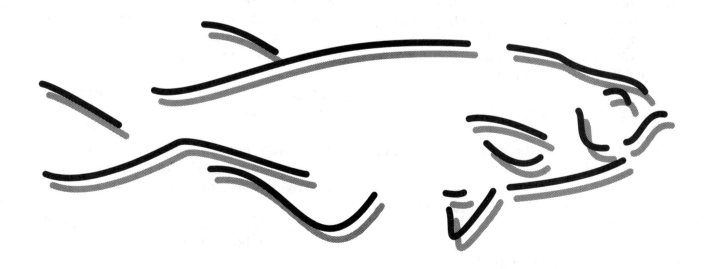

SIN GAME

by Randall & Arinée Glass, and J. Scott Reynolds

Satan enjoys hosting the game that he invented

Purpose: *To show the consequences of sin*

Adapted from: *Galatians 6:7*

Cast:
Satan
Sweet Talking Suzie: plays game of gossip
Jack O. Daniel: plays game of alcohol
Ms. Immo Rality: plays game of adultery
Announcer

Props: *Dice, table for dice, cue cards for **Satan***

Announcer: Welcome ladies and gentlemen to the oldest game in the world—the *"Sin Game"* — where you can risk your *own* life *and* the lives of *others*! With our host — Satan, the quicker tripper upper! *(Satan enters.)*

Satan: Welcome! Welcome! Now in this game all you have to do is tell me which sin game you want to play, then you roll the dice and get your prize. You can either keep that prize or give up that prize and try for a *better* prize! You can stop whenever you want! You only get three rolls. And now for our first contestant— Sweet Talking Suzie, come on down!

Suzie: Oh, I'm so excited!

Satan: OK, Sweet Talking Suzie, what's the game you want to play?

Suzie: Umm, I think "Gossiping About Church Members!"

Satan: All right, that sounds like a good one to me! You know the rules!

Suzie: Yes!

Satan: All right, roll the dice!

Suzie rolls the dice. When they land she jumps up and down.

Satan: On your first roll you got *popularity*! Do you want to roll again? Of course you do! Roll again Suzie! *(Suzie rolls again.)* Oh Suzie, I am so sorry, this time you got a few people in the church mad at you. That's too bad. But you have one more roll so you can get a much better prize! And I know you want to roll again, so roll it Suzie! *(She rolls the dice.)* Oh no, Suzie— because of this gossip game you caused your church to split. Oh, well! Better luck next time!

Suzie: You mean that's my prize — my church ruined? That's it? This isn't fair!

Satan: Bye, bye, Suzie! Thanks for playing games with your life! *(Suzie exits. Jack enters.)* Now our next contestant — Mr. Jack O. Daniel. OK, Jack, tell us what is the sin game you're wanting to play with your life?

Jack: Yes, I'd like to play the sin game of "Substance Abuse!"

Satan: Great, I like this one! We've got some great prizes for you Jack, I'm sure! You know the rules, right? Okay, roll 'em!

Jack: *(rolls dice)* Yeah, Yeah! I'm the life of the party — everybody loves me! I have a blast!

Satan: That's right, Jack. You got a pretty good

prize there — but I know there's got to be a better one for you. You do want to roll again, right Jack?

Jack: I don't know, I rolled . . .

Satan: That's right Jack, roll again.

Jack: Well, I think I'll just keep . . .

Satan: Roll again, Jack — you can't stop now! *(Jack rolls again.)* See that, Jack, you got rid of all your problems!

Jack: That's a great prize — no more problems! I've gotta roll again — who knows what else I could get!

Satan: Roll again, Jack. This is your last roll. *(Jack rolls dice.)*

Satan: Oh darn, Jack — you just lost your job. And you're addicted to this game — you can never quit this substance abuse game, ever. Oh, well. Don't worry, be happy!

Jack: You mean my job is down the drain and I'm an addict? What kind of prize is *that*?

Satan: That's just one of the many prizes we have on the show! Thanks Jack — have a great life! *(He laughs. **Jack** exits. **Immo** enters.)* Now for our next contestant. Ms. Immo Rality please come on down!

Immo: Just call me Immo.

Satan: Okay, name your poison, or uh, your game.

Immo: I want to play "Adulterous Scandalous Affairs!"

Satan: Okay! So, do you have a husband and a family?

Immo: Yeah, I have a husband and three kids.

Satan: Oh, so you're risking a lot aren't you? I

like that! Well, let's get started. Ms. Rality or Immo, you know the rules so let's go — roll the dice!

Immo: *(She rolls the dice.)* Yeah! I got a lot of mystery and excitement! This is a fun game!

Satan: Now roll again — you have two more rolls, Ms. Immo Rality.

Immo: You said at the beginning of the game that we could stop whenever we want, so I think I'll stop right here and take my prize.

Satan: Oh, did I say that? Well, I lied. You have to take all of your rolls Ms. Immo.

Immo: But that's not fair.

Satan: Did I say it was? Now you got two more.

Immo: *(She rolls the dice.)* Oh no, I just lost my family — my husband divorces me and takes the children! I don't like this game.

Satan: Oh, but you liked your first roll didn't you? Sometimes you have to risk a lot to get what you want. But, you have one more roll Ms. Rality.

Immo: Maybe this will be a better prize. *(She rolls.)* AIDS? I've got AIDS!?

Satan: That's right, Ms. Immo Rality! Thanks for being on the show. What prizes we have on this show! Our time is up today, but just remember, you could be the next contestant on the *"Sin Game!"* Where you risk your life and the lives of others!

Announcer: That's right, Ladies and Gentlemen, you too could be on the *"Sin Game"* show — just choose *your* sin game and get ready to reap what you sow!!

THE SEARCH

by Leigh Ann Thomas

Great sketch for women's ministry!

Cast: *Woman 1* and *Woman 2*

Setting: *The two women may be standing together or on opposite sides of the stage.*

Woman 1: I had just graduated from high school. What a wonderful time that was! . . . a fresh start with no one to hold me back or tell me how to run my life. Adults in my life had failed, but not me . . . I knew what the answer was . . .

Woman 2: Education. I knew there was no problem that couldn't be solved with education.

Woman 1: So I went to college and started really enjoying all that life had to offer. I studied under brilliant professors who were 10 times smarter than my stone-aged parents would ever be . . .

Woman 2: I came face to face with the truth . . . that strength, happiness, and peace came from within . . . and that my success or failure was entirely up to me.

Woman 1: I had the power to control my destiny and shape the course of my life . . . the only problem was . . .

Woman 2: I wasn't happy . . . brilliance was great, but I needed someone to share it with . . .

Woman 1: So I went to all the best parties, and I concentrated on meeting those men I knew were going somewhere . . .

Woman 2: I dated anyone who was wealthy and had ambition. I knew where happiness was, and it wasn't living in poverty . . .

Woman 1: After graduation, I married a wonderful man . . . strong, ambitious . . . a born leader. Together we would conquer the world . . .

Woman 2: We threw ourselves into our careers and we began to accumulate a lot of possessions. The American dream was finally ours . . . the only problem was . . .

Woman 1: . . . our house never seemed quite big enough and things we acquired never seemed to satisfy, and the years of concentrating on our careers were beginning to take a toll on our marriage.

Woman 2: Our beautiful house just wasn't a home. I felt that something was missing, but I just couldn't put my finger on what it was . . .

Woman 1: I had to do something to save our marriage . . . so we had children . . . what a joy! . . . I had finally found some sense of fulfillment . . .

Woman 2: But it didn't help my marriage . . . we became two strangers sharing the same living space . . .

Woman 1: But that didn't matter . . . I had the children . . . I quit my job and threw myself into motherhood. No matter what, I was there for them . . . school, sports, clubs . . . I became totally absorbed in their lives . . .

Woman 2: I was so busy. I didn't have time to think . . . to examine *my* life . . .

Woman 1: As the years went by, I became more and more lonely. The children had their friends and my husband was married to his career . . .

Woman 2: *(sarcastically)* Then a friend told me that I was lacking a "spiritual" dimension to my life, so I began searching . . .

Woman 1: . . . but there were so many voices . . . everyone had the answers, but they were all different. Looking within and depending on myself wasn't enough anymore . . .

Woman 2: So I joined a local church and threw myself into every activity offered . . .

Woman 1: I taught Sunday School, worked with the youth, and joined all the ladies' groups . . .

Woman 2: My life was full of activity . . .

Woman 1: But no peace.

Woman 2: And now I stand here and look at you all sitting here . . . in a church of all places . . . and I have to laugh . . . Am I bitter? Yeah, maybe . . . but can you blame me? I just feel so cheated . . . I've tried everything this world has to offer . . . and I've gained nothing.

Woman 1: I tried religion . . . and gained nothing.

Woman 2: I feel cold and unattached . . . without hope or a sense of purpose . . .

Woman 1: Tell me, am I wrong? . . . am I missing something here?

THE WATCHMAN
by Christopher Morelock

Excellent material to challenge and promote your prayer ministry

Cast: *Biblical Watchman, Contemporary Man*

Adapted from: *Isaiah 62*

Trumpet sounds (live or recorded)

Watchman: Hear my voice, O Jerusalem. I, the watchman have seen the enemy and we must prepare! For the day of the Lord is come. For Zion's sake I will not keep silent. For Jerusalem's sake I will not remain quiet. Till her righteousness shines out like the dawn. Her salvation like a blazing torch! *(pause)*

I am the watchman who has been posted on your walls, Jerusalem. I have sounded the warning cry for all to hear. Ye who have ears to hear stand with me and prepare for battle! For the enemy is at our door. By the power of the almighty, arm yourselves with armor and with swords and stand and fight with me! *(pause)*

Why do you sit there so complacently? Why do you go about with your ordinary lives and not heed the call? There is a battle raging outside that door. There are lives being stalked, the enemy is upon our heels! Why do you not stand? How can you hear and not respond? Have you become bound by the enemy without a fight? Look! The army is coming. They are armed with swords and spears. They are cruel and they show no mercy. They sound like the roaring sea as they ride upon their horses. And they come to attack you, O daughter of Zion! *(pause)*

Isaiah posted watchman on your walls, Jerusalem, and said, "Listen to the sound of the trumpets." But you said, "We will not listen!" Therefore, hear me, O earth! The Lord God bringeth disaster upon this people, the fruit of their schemes, for they have not listened to His words and have rejected His law! Therefore if no man, if no man under heaven and earth will stand up and fight for his Lord — *pause* — we will surely perish.

Contemporary Man: You know the watchman is right in his warning to us. We, as Christians, have become complacent in our everyday lives. We have given up our Christian freedoms by surrendering to the demands of a Godless society. *(beat)* However there is a way we can free ourselves from the influences of the world. Prayer. We must get on our knees and guard against the attack of the enemy. James 5:16 says "The prayer of a righteous man is powerful and effective." *(NIV)*

(pause)

The solution is so simple. Just pray. When was the last time you prayed for your country? When was the last time you prayed for your church? Your neighbors? Your family? Or even yourself? When was the last time you felt your spirit renewed? The time has come for us to become watchmen for our church. The only way we can protect ourselves from the enemy is through prayer. Will we sit in the pews comfortably and watch other people perish? Or will we get down on our knees and commit ourselves to prayer? The choice is ours.

PEACE WITH AN "A"

by Nancy Sheffey

A monologue on stress

Cast: *Career Woman*

Setting: *A typical, power-dressed **Career Woman** is putting her papers angrily into her leather attache for another weekend of work.*

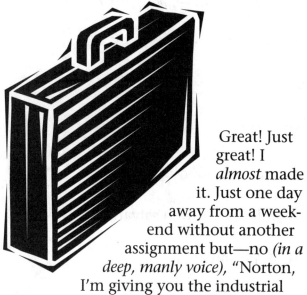

Great! Just great! I *almost* made it. Just one day away from a weekend without another assignment but—no *(in a deep, manly voice),* "Norton, I'm giving you the industrial park piece. With your contacts and efficiency, I'm sure you can have it on my desk by Monday morning." *(sarcastically)* Such flattery, Mr. Swenson, such praise, *(building)* such accolades! *(low voice, full of anger)* "She's only been here eight months—stick her with the piece." So it's *my* piece. My *piece* of the action. My *piece* of the rock. *(through clenched teeth)* My *piece* of the pie! And another weekend eludes me. Why am I always crawling toward them like some dying man in the desert crawls toward a mirage? *(She continues as she puts on her overcoat to leave.)* Maybe that's what it is — a mirage. I mean, whatever happened to peace with an "a." *(strong—directly to audience)* Is it reality or just a word we use?

World peace. Greenpeace. Peace in the Middle East. Peace, love, Woodstock. *(building)* Peace on earth. Peace time! *Is there such a thing? (voice low)* I have neither. *(She is emotional, dejected. She closes the attache as she says . . .)* I've had it. *(Her lips are quivering. She seems almost at the breaking point. She stands dejected, case at her side, her voice trembling.)* I know what I have to do. *(pause—then with resolve)* I've got to get a car phone and a beeper. It's the only thing. *(This perks her up and she's off again.)* I know people who have them and it's doubled their productivity. I mean, accessibility is the key in time management. That way, my people could get in touch with me anytime of the day— and with more time I can take more yoga classes, change my mantra and go to 40— no . . . 50 minutes on the treadmill!! YES!! *(Starts off, turns abruptly to audience.) This could work for me!*

45

HIS NAME

by Deborah P. Brunt

Try using this as a dramatic bridge to musical worship

Cast: *Voice of Jesus, Soprano, Alto, Tenor, Bass voices*

Soprano: He sat at the table with His disciples.

Alto: He was calm; the disciples, troubled.

Jesus: "Do not let your hearts be troubled. Trust in God; trust also in me. In my Father's house are many rooms; if it were not so, I would have told you. *I am going there* to prepare a place for you. And if I go and prepare a place for you, I will come back and take you to be with me that you also may be where I am. You know the way to the place where I am going.

Bass: *(bewildered)* "Lord, we don't know where you are going, so how can we know the way?

Jesus: "*I am* the way and the truth and the life. No one comes to the Father except through me.

Tenor: *(eagerly)* "Lord, show us the Father and that will be enough for us.

Jesus: *(with great intensity)* "Don't you know me, even after I have been among you such a long time? Anyone who has seen me has seen the Father." *(John 14:1-9, part, NIV)*

Women: The Father

Men: Yahweh

All: I AM

Women: The Son

Men: Jesus, Yahweh salvation

All: I AM salvation.

Alto: I AM all the Father is.

Soprano: I AM all the Father requires.

Tenor: I AM all any person needs.

Bass: I AM

All: Jesus.

Segue into the choir or a choral group singing a song like "His Name," "No Other Name," or "How Excellent Is Thy Name"

REMOTE CONTROL

by Claire Hamilton

A sketch to illustrate the concepts of mercy and apathy

Cast: *Nine People (male or female)*

Props: *One chair & a TV remote control*

Setting: *Person enters, sits, and begins watching TV. He should change channels after each of the eight actors enters. After a brief pause, the first actor enters, stands to one side.*

#1: *(reaching out)* I was hungry.

(# 2 enters, stands opposite of #1.)

#2: *(reaching out)* I was thirsty.

(# 3 enters, stands opposite of # 2.)

#3: *(looking down)* I was a stranger.

(#4 enters, stands opposite of #3.)

#4: *(humble)* I was in need of clothes.

(#5 enters, stands opposite of #4.)

#5: *(weakly)* I was sick.

(#6 enters, stands opposite of #5.)

#6: *(despair)* I was in prison.

(#7 enters, stands opposite of #6.)

 # 7: *(edgy)* I was your co-worker . . . hurting and you never asked . . . not once.

(#8 enters, stands opposite of #7.)

#8: *(lonely)* I was sitting beside you in the pew. You never took my hand.

Person *continues to watch TV as all eight reach out to different levels . . . Freeze.*

WHAT'S IN THE BOX?

by Christal Hughes

Salvation is free — just receive it

Cast: *Four people, male or female*

Props: *A large gift-wrapped box, which has written on it in large letters*
"Paid in Full, Very High Price, for You"

Setting: *The large gift is in the center of the stage. Each of the first three persons walks by the gift, choosing not to accept it. The last person finally takes it.*

Person 1: *(walks by the gift)* Wow! Would you look at that. This looks so nice. *(Reads the message on the box.)* Oh . . . I get it . . . very high price . . . that means it will probably cost me something. No way . . . I'm not falling for that one . . . there's no such thing as a free gift. *(Walks of.f)*

Person 2: *(Walks by the gift in a hurry, catches a glimpse of the gift, stops abruptly.)* What's this? Great looking gift. *(Reads message on box.)* Looks like it's just for me. *(Looks at watch.)* But I don't really have time right now . . . I have so much to do first. I'll get it later. *(Walks off fast.)*

Person 3: *(Walks by gift.)* This is so nice. *(Reads the message on the gift.)* But . . . I didn't do anything for it . . . I mean, I know it says "free" . . . but there must be something I'm supposed to do to *earn* it. Or maybe I could buy it. It can't be as simple as just receiving it. *(Shakes head and walks away.)*

Person 4: *(Walks by the gift, stops and reads it aloud.)* I've been waiting for this all my life. *(Opens the gift and takes out a piece of paper, turns toward the audience and reads.)* "For the wages of sin is death, but the gift of God is eternal life in Christ Jesus our Lord." *(Rom. 6:23, NIV)*

GIFTS

by Jean Beasley

Spiritual Gifts: giving what you receive...

*As lights come up, **Recipients 1**, **2**, and **3** are sitting around a mound of torn wrapping paper (not Christmas paper), ribbons, gift tags, cards, boxes, etc., but no merchandise of any sort is evident. There are also a number of unopened gifts beside **Recipient 3**. These three people should be adults, not children or youth, in order to make their childish behavior as incongruous, and as grating, as possible.*

Recipient 1: *(picking up a card and reading from it)* Listen to this: "Each man has his own gift from God." *(1Cor. 7:7) (throwing the card down peevishly)* How personal! You know, He *still* hasn't sent me what I asked for!

Recipient 2: *(also picking up a card)* How about this one: "Do not neglect your gift." *(1 Tim. 4:14) (ripping card in half)* I was always taught not to give a person something that would put any demands on them, like plants, or pets, or . . . *that*!

Recipient 3: *(picking up one of his/her unopened packages and reading from it's tag)* Well, listen to mine: "Each one should use whatever gift he has received to serve others." *(1 Pet. 4:10)* Talk about a gift that puts demands on you! And this one: *(reading from a card)* "God's gifts . . . are irrevocable."

Recipient 1: We'll see about that! *(having a classic temper tantrum)* I'm gonna exchange this for something *I* want!

Recipient 3: *(Paws through the debris and picks out cards; throwing a wadded-up ball of wrapping paper at Recipient 1.)* This must have been one of yours: "If a man's gift is prophesying, let him use it in proportion to his faith. If it is serving, let him serve; if it is teaching, let him teach. . . ." *(Rom. 12: 6-7)*

Recipient 2: So we can't use each other's gifts? That's not fair! *(punching at **Recipient 1** to stop the tantrum)* Hey, I know! Let's trade! I'll give you this *(waving a box around)* for . . . *(grabbing two larger boxes from the edge of the pile closest to **Recipient 1**)* these!

Recipient 1: I get one and you get two? No fair!

Recipient 2: Take it or leave it.

Recipient 1: Oh, alright! *(peevishly exchanges gifts with **Recipient 2** and sits pouting)*

Recipient 3: Who's was this? "Now about spiritual gifts, brothers, I do not want you to be ignorant." *(1 Cor. 12:1) (whining)* He's always giving us something *educational*! Oh, here's a good one: "But eagerly desire the greater gifts." *(1 Cor. 12:31)* And this is just like that last one: "Since you are eager to have spiritual gifts, try to excel in gifts that build up the church." *(1 Cor. 14:12)*

Recipient 2: Yeah, those were mine. *(kicking at the pile of debris)* He gives me *that* and tells me to *want* other stuff!

Recipient 3: *(putting the trash **Recipient 2** has kicked aside back on the pile)* Stop it! We have to clean this up and you're just making it worse! Besides, you'll probably get the greater gifts next time.

Recipient 1: Oh, yeah? You didn't read that whole card before, did you? *I* know, because He sent *me* the same one last time. *(**Recipients 1** and **3** tussle over the card in question; **Recipient 1** ends up with it.)* Uh-huh . . . here it is: "Are all apostles? Are all prophets? Are all teachers? Do all work miracles? Do all have gifts of healing? " *(1 Cor. 12:29)* Blah, blah, blah.

Recipient 2: Yeah, and *then* it says, "But eagerly desire the greater gifts!" *(1 Cor. 12:31)* So, in other words, we're not *all* going to *get* the greater gifts . . . ever!

Recipient 1: That's right!

Recipient 3: Maybe, maybe not. You don't know!

Recipient 2: *(glaring at **Recipient 3**)* Then who's got 'em?

Recipient 1: *(also glaring at **Recipient 3**)* Gee, I wonder! *(advancing on **Recipient 3**)* 'Fess up!

Recipient 2: Hand 'em over!

*The three scuffle for a minute, while **Recipients 1** and **2** adlib comments like "Say 'uncle'!" and trash flies everywhere.*

Recipient 3: Uncle! Get off me — I *said* "uncle!"

Recipient 1: *(panting)* Where are the greater gifts?

Recipient 3: I don't know.

Recipient 2: *(sarcastically)* Well, where did you put them?

Recipient 3: *(straightening hair and clothes)* I *mean*, I don't even know if I got them!

Recipient 1: Come off it! Just because you won't open your gifts in front of *us* . . . *(kicking **Recipient 3**)* doesn't mean you *never* open them! How stupid do you think we are?

Recipient 3: *(kicking back)* I haven't opened them yet!

Recipient 2: None of them? *(as **Recipient 3** shakes his head "no")* Right!

Recipient 3: I haven't gotten around to it!

Recipient 1: You just don't want to have to *do* anything with your gifts!

Recipient 3: No, I never said that . . .

Recipient 1: So what! It's true!

Recipient 3: Well, so what if it is! At least I don't try to *trade* my gifts, or exchange them . . .

Recipient 1: Big deal!

Recipient 2: *(as **Recipients 1** and **3** start exchanging blows)* Uh, guys . . . did you hear something just now . . . some kind of . . . there! Hear it?

Recipient 3: *(scooting away from Recipient 1)* Hear what?

All react as if they've heard a frightening sound.

Recipient 2: THAT!

All scurry to clean up.

Recipient 1: *(panicked)* Where are the thank-you cards?

Recipient 3: We don't have time for that now! *(thrusting some of his unopened gifts at the others)* Quick! Open something and *use* it!

Recipient 2: *(ripping into one)* He's not going to be very happy! You know how He likes to see how we've enjoyed our gifts, made something out of them . . .

Recipient 1: *(after looking into the box Recipient 3 gave him)* This is no good! He picked this especially for you—He'll notice!

Recipient 3: Well, hurry up and find yours, then!

*Recipients **1** and **2** root frantically through the pile for a few seconds, freezing with fake smiles on their faces as Recipient 3 continues, looking at a spot above the audience's heads.*

Recipient 3: *(nervously)* He . . . hello, Father! We didn't expect you back so soon. *(with obviously fake enthusiasm)* Nice gifts!

All scriptures are from the *NIV* version.

FEARFUL EARFUL

by Rich Peterson

Good sermon starter on fear

Setting: A beauty salon. There are three women sitting in chairs with solid color hair caps on their heads. There are three hair dressers—two are doing nails, one is doing toenails. Gladys, Pidge (toenails) and Munroe are the hairdressers. Inge, Stu, and Wallace are the three women being "done."

Gladys: *(doing Inge's nails)* How's that, Inge?

Inge: Fine, Gladys. But be careful of the little one. I'm afraid it'll fall out.

Gladys: Ooops! It did. I'm so sorry!

Inge: I knew it! Can you put in a new one?

Gladys: Nothing that a little bondo can't fix, dear.

Pidge: Can you lift up your second toe, Stu? I can't quite get it.

Stu: *(she does)* Sure Pidge, How's that?

Pidge: Fine. Fine. Say—are you thinkin' about going into the mission field? I know you wanted to.

Stu: With these flat feet? I don't think so. Besides I hear there are tigers in India who eat feet for breakfast. And with what you're charging me for this pedicure, that's an expensive meal!

Pidge: So you don't want to go to India because you're afraid of the tigers? Thought you felt called.

Stu: My toes don't feel called to be tiger chow.

Pidge: Ah, de agony of de feet!

Stu: Save it, Pidge — Oooh watch it! You always poke me.

Pidge: Sorry. Catbite!

Stu: It's not funny. I want to go—but I'm afraid, all right?

Pidge: They say the thing you fear is the very thing that happens to you.

Stu: That's exactly what I mean!

Wallace: I'm going bald—I just know it!

Munroe: Now Mrs. Wallace. You say that every time you come in here.

Wallace: I know but it's just getting worse and worse. My sons gave me a wash cloth to part my hair with!

Stu: Ouch!

Pidge: Sorry.

Munroe: Nonsense. You have a fine head of hair.

Pidge: What happened here?

Stu: I stubbed my toe.

Pidge: What happened?

Stu: I'm afraid of the dark, All right? My sweety-nite light went out last night and I woke up in a cold sweat. I stepped out of bed and I thought I heard something downstairs. That's when I stepped on the clock.

Pidge: The clock?

Stu: I'm afraid that I won't get up if the alarm goes off by my bed, so I set it in the middle of the room.

Pidge: So—you stubbed your toe on the clock.

Stu: No — I stubbed it on the rock.

Pidge: *(stops working)* The rock?

Stu: That I keep by my bed by my clock.

Stu and Pidge together: In case *(I) (you)*

hear someone downstairs.

Pidge: I see.

Inge: I used to be afraid of being too tall.

Gladys: Now being tall is in.

Inge: Now I'm afraid of being too short.

Wallace: I'm afraid my kids won't graduate, I'm afraid I'm overweight, I'm afraid I'll get a divorce, and I'm afraid I'll go bald.

Munroe: Is there anything you're not afraid of?

Wallace: I'm afraid not.

Gladys, Pidge and Munroe: We're done! Time to check your hair color!

Inge, Stu and Wallace: We're afraid of what color it's going to be!

Wallace: And I'm afraid of going bald!

The hairdressers pull off the haircaps and Inge has green hair, Stu has orange hair, and Wallace is bald as a billiard ball!

Inge, Stu and Wallace: *(scream and run out!)*

Gladys, Pidge and Munroe: Maybe it was something we said? *(to congregation)* 'Fraid not!!! *(ad lib as they exit)* Hey come back here! Why are you running away? Come back! We'll try again! *(etc.)*

MARY'S LAMENT

by Christy Marsh Haines

Easter Sunday worship addition

Mary, the mother of Jesus, sits alone on a bench early on Sunday morning, after the crucifixion, before the resurrection. Keening, wistful, remembering, angry, hopeful, stream of consciousness. It is very effective if Mary is dressed totally in black, with her face and hands made up with a Mediterranean look. The hands (also made up) can be used quite expressively, using the black background of the robe to help them stand out.

Oh, my son, my son. You knew it would come to this. I did, too, but I still don't want to accept it! *(transition)* I didn't sleep again last night. The treasures I have hidden in my heart for so long are little comfort to me now. To be chosen to be the mother of the Son of God was something I could not fully comprehend. Yet you, my son, you led me, gave me the faith to see it through. When you were a tiny baby, and we took you to the temple to be dedicated, old Simeon held you in his arms and said that you would be the greatest joy of many, as you have been to me. But that you would be rejected by many. *(transition)* How could they reject you? You were love! And all knowledge. And all wisdom. *(transition)* When you were just a boy, the elders in the temple sat at your feet and listened, because you taught as one who had authority! I was so proud of you! *(transition)* We had such a special relationship. When you were little, I would hold you in my arms and heal your physical wounds. And then you grew, and

you would hold me in your arms and heal my spiritual wounds. *(transition)* How could they reject you?! Couldn't they see that you only loved? You didn't come to lead an insurrection! You didn't come to harm! You came with healing in your hands. You would gently touch the crooked back of an old woman, and she would stand up straight again. You grasped the unclean leper and cleansed him from his disease. You commanded the man in the dirt to take up his bed and walk! You even loved the unlovable, lepers...prostitutes...thieves. *(transition) The* thief. When I knelt at your feet and looked up and saw your bleeding and broken body, I wanted to take you in my arms once again and heal your wounds. But you. You, even in your last agony, you thought of me! To take care of me! *(transition)* When Simeon told me that a sword would pierce my soul, I didn't know it would hurt so much! *(transition)* I had bought herbs to rub on your tortured body, though you wouldn't feel my touch. But I couldn't bring myself to go to the tomb. So the others have gone in my place. *(transition)* You told me you would come again, but I can't see it! Lord, help my unbelief! *(transition; an unseen Mary Magdalene enters)* Magdalene, Magdalene...what is it, my child? *(Mary "listens" while Magdalene tells her of her experience at the tomb. Mary's crying turns to laughter, and she rises and shouts!)* HE IS RISEN! *(Mary exits quickly, running to the empty tomb.)*

FORGOTTEN BATTLES

by Christy Doyle

A Memorial Day remembrance

Setting: *A woman is sitting on a lawn chair with a small flag.*

Memorial Day is a strange holiday, isn't it? It's a day when we're supposed to sit back and remember all those people who have died in wars. But, in reality, Memorial Day is known more for its barbecues and picnics than its long-forgotten battles.

It seems like such a long, long time ago that my big brother went to Vietnam. He was 10 years older than I and the best brother that ever lived. He'd take me to the movies and even let me play his records. He used to call me "Little Sis" . . . "Hey, Little Sis" . . . And I'd call him "Duke" because he used to love those old John Wayne movies. Even after all these years, I still have flashes of "Dukie." It's the love I remember. I guess that's what you always remember.

Recently I went to the Wall to look for his name. I was overwhelmed with emotion as I touched his name. . . . And as I stood there my hand dropped down to another name and my heart jumped. There was the name "Jesus." Some mother had named her little boy, "Jesus." There was the name of the Lord amongst all the pain and the suffering. And then I thought about all the battles we go through in life. When we lost Duke, my dad never got over it. And I cried because I wanted my brother back—never realizing that Jesus, my adopted brother, was there all the time.

Boy, life seems to be one battle after another. You know, Duke was a great soldier because he fought until the very end. Sometimes I'm scared I won't make it to the end. But then I remember Jesus and the battle He fought on the cross. Duke was in a lost and forgotten war, but I'm not—because Jesus died for me. You know, I've always been someone who didn't want to look at death. But when I think of Duke and Jesus, it gives me the courage to hang on.

Maybe Memorial Day isn't so strange. I guess we do need to remember those forgotten battles. After all, if we didn't remember Calvary . . . well, we'd be fighting a losing battle.

COMING, READY OR NOT

by Gail Blanton

A parable of being prepared to meet your maker

Cast: *Janice*, *Voice* (visible at end)

Janice is seated in front of a mirror. She is preparing to go out but is obviously a long way from being ready. Her belt and shoes lie on the floor. Her blouse is misbuttoned and not tucked in. There are a couple of rollers still in her hair and various items of jewelry and makeup lie on the dressing table. She continues dressing, making up, etc. during the dialogue, but is still quite obviously unprepared by the end. Voice is off-stage until the last line; then appears as a figure in a black robe with a death mask or hood that hides his face. He speaks in a normal voice; no hint of the sinister; audience should assume it is an impatient husband. Although his impatience builds throughout, it should not indicate anger, only a determined, indisputable power.

Voice: Come on, Janice.

Janice: I'm not ready yet.

Voice: Well it's time to go.

Janice: It couldn't be time already.

Voice: But it is.

Janice: Oh, quit your kidding around. It couldn't possibly be time yet.

Voice: You know I don't kid around. Come on.

Janice: Will you stop shouting across to me? Come in here and wait, or sit down and relax. I haven't finished doing my hair. I haven't done my nails, my eyes—

Voice: Then you'll just have to leave them. Come on now. It's time to go.

Janice: It is not. *(muttering; almost to herself)*

Voice: I don't intend to argue with you. Get out here.

Janice: Hey, who do you think you're talking to, Buster?

Voice: You, Sister. We've not had a confrontation lately and you may not remember, but I am not by any means patient.

Janice: And I am not by any means ready.

Voice: That's your problem. You've had plenty of time. When I say "move" you know you'd better move.

Janice: *(changing tactics)* Oh, don't be such a meanie. I might make it worth your wait. Why don't you come in here and talk to me while I —

Voice: Get out here, I said!

Janice: Oh, all right. Wait till I get these rollers out of my hair. Just a minute.

Voice: Now!

Janice: *(changing tactics again)* Well, I'm just not going, then.

Voice: Oh yes, you are going. And we're leaving this instant. Do I make myself clear?

Janice: *(Rises quickly, muttering; fumbles with shoes as this line is delivered.)* I'm not even half ready.

Voice: *(as figure steps into the room and grabs Janice's arm)* Then you'll have to go just as you are — ready or not.

BLACKOUT

CHOICES

by Debra Crawley

Short seeker script on the breakup of the home

Setting: *Debra and John's living room*

*Debra enters the room as **John** is gathering his personal belongings.*

Debra: I thought you'd be gone by the time I got back.

John: I'll be out of here in a couple of minutes.

Debra: Good. The sooner, the better.

John: Yeah, for both of us.

Debra: "For both of us?" Since when have you ever considered *both* of us?

John: Oh, please! Do we have to go into all of this again? We've played this scene over and over.

Debra: Don't worry. After tonight, you'll never have to listen to my "nagging" voice again. As soon as you're out of that door, you're out of my life and I'm out of yours . . . forever! It's that easy, isn't it?

John: I wonder if anything is really ever that easy. *(looking around)* Where are the kids?

Debra: At Beth's. I didn't want them here for this.

John: Yeah. I don't want them here either . . . not now, like this. Can I see them next week? I miss them already.

Debra: You should have thought about a long time ago.

John: Look. What else do you want me to say? I've tried and tried, but it doesn't get any better. I cannot live here under all of this pressure anymore. I have no other choice.

Debra: Choices? Don't talk to me about choices. You made yours.

John: And so did you.

Debra: Well, maybe I wasn't given much of an alternative.

John: And maybe you didn't look for one very hard.

Debra: Maybe I didn't want to . . . But it takes two to make a relationship work.

John: We just don't seem to be able to meet each other halfway, do we?

Debra: I don't think that you've ever really tried.

John: Don't start in on me again. You know that I've tried. It was just never good enough for you.

Debra: I . . . *(changing the subject)* Well . . . it doesn't matter now. It's too late.

John: What are you going to tell the children?

Debra: I don't know. But I'll come up with something. I'll handle it. I *always* do.

John: Well, whatever. *(pauses for a moment trying to think of something else to say)* Anything else??

Segue to solo "God Has Another Plan," (by Babbie Mason, Word, 1992).

THE PEACE THAT PASSES

by Nancy Sheffey

A series of five vignettes that could be performed separately or interspersed with music

"Peace I leave with you; My peace I give to you; not as the world gives do I give to you. Let not your heart be troubled, nor let it be fearful" (John 14:27, NASB).

"And the peace of God, which surpasses all comprehension, shall guard your hearts and your minds in Christ Jesus" (Phil. 4:7, NASB).

Steve, Larry and Carlyle are three middle-age men, talking during a coffee break at work.

Larry: Frank said Dylan got pink-slipped and he's a 13-year man. It's coming, Steve. I know it. Fifteen years with this company and what do I get?

Steve: Fifteen? I've got 17—and a kid in college and my ex is screaming for more child support.

Larry: I hear Tanex is hiring.

Steve: Management only. I know two guys that tried it. How many years you got, Carlyle?

Carlyle: Eighteen.

Steve: I guess we'll go first, then. You got any savings, Larry?

Larry: Not much. The wife's got a couple of C.D.'s, but that was for retirement.

Steve: *(with anger)* Ha! What retirement? We won't even get a gold watch to hock! We got nothin' but bills and debt. I'd like to put a big hurt on Shamblee for this.

Larry: *(to Carlyle)* How 'bout you, Wayne? How're you gonna do?

Carlyle: *(with assurance)* Just fine, Larry. I'll do just fine.

Larry: You win the lottery and didn't tell us?

Carlyle: *(smiling)* No. Got a little put back.

Steve: *(bitter)* A little, huh? How long is a little gonna last these days?

Carlyle: Long enough.

Larry: *(confused)* You're not worried?

Steve: *(gruffly)* Anything ever rile you, Carlyle?

Carlyle: I *could* worry, Steve, but I won't. I got a promise a long time ago that everything that happens to me is for my good.

Steve: *(sarcastically)* That include gettin' laid off?

Larry: After 18 years?

Carlyle: *(explains gently)* I look at it like this. I can't see down the road I'm travelin'. I can't even see around the corner. Can you? Can any of us? Maybe I *will* get laid off. Maybe I'll have to move, be forced to try something else—maybe start my own business. Jackie and I have talked about it. And maybe it'll be better than this. Better than we ever dreamed. The best is yet to come—you ever think of that? This could be the best thing that could happen to me. I don't know what the future holds, but I know who holds the future.

Steve: Yeah? Who?

Carlyle: The same one who promised that everything that happens in it is for my good.

*Two teenagers are studying together: **Sandy** and **Denise**.*

Sandy: If I blow this test, my parents are gonna kill me.

Denise: What are you talking about?

Sandy: Scholarship, dear. They've been talking the "S" word as long as I can remember.

Denise: *(reassuring her)* You've got the grades.

Sandy: Yeah, but without the SAT's, I can kiss it good-by.

Denise: You'll do great.

Sandy: That's what you always say.

Denise: *(teasing)* And I'm always right!

Sandy: *(exasperated with her)* But this is the SAT, Denise! You know what these mean! What about you? My parents can pay for med school three times over but — you — well, no offense — but it's just your mom. You've worked as hard as I have — you gotta have a scholarship even to go to state, and you're not even nervous!

Denise: Sandy, if it's God's plan for me to go to college — I'll go.

Sandy: How?

Denise: I don't know.

Sandy: You don't know?

Denise: But He does. I trust Him.

Sandy: I don't get you, "Nise." We've been friends a long time — in the same youth group forever. I'm a Christian too, but I'm gonna die of an ulcer before I'm 25 — and you — cool and calm — will bury me!

✝ ✝ ✝ ✝

*A **Doctor**, fresh out of surgery, enters and goes to **Wife**, waiting with her teenage **Son**.*

Doctor: *(Goes to **Wife**, speaks in a low voice, trying to get her alone.)* I think . . . uh . . . we need to talk, Mrs. Franklin.

Wife: It's O.K. Doctor. *Ttakes **Son**'s hand to show they are together in this.)* You can tell us—both.

Doctor: *(skeptical, haltingly)* All right . . . It is worse than we anticipated. Your husband has suffered a myocardial infarction which has caused what we call ischemia [is-keem'-ia] to the posterior cardiac wall. His heart is damaged beyond repair.

Son: *(anxious)* You mean you can't fix it?

Doctor: No. *(to **Wife**)* The prognosis is not good, Mrs. Franklin.

Wife: What *can* you do? *(She is calm, her voice steady.)*

Dr: In a case like this we can only hope to maintain your husband —

Son: *(interrupting)* What about diet and exercise? My dad's only 41!

Doctor: They can't help this heart — it has sustained too much damage. *(to Wife)* With digitalis and some beta blockers we will be doing well to keep Mr. Franklin alive. He can't survive another heart attack, however mild.

Wife: How long can he live with these drugs?

Doctor: *(takes deep breath)* His only chance for long term survival is another heart.

Wife: A . . . transplant?

Doctor: Yes.

Wife: *(Leans back, looks at son.)* Then that's what we'll ask for. *(back to Doctor)* When can we see him?

Doctor: *(bewildered at her reaction, thinking she doesn't grasp the gravity of the situation)* When he's stable on the monitor we'll call you, but your visits will have to be very brief.

Wife: Thank you, Doctor. I know you've done all you can. *(She turns to her son, who sits beside her gazing away in thought.)*

Doctor: *(feeling she hasn't understood the seriousness of her husband's plight, tries again)* Mrs. Franklin, I want you to understand. Your husband is gravely ill. The situation is very unstable. There are no guarantees with this. Transplantation is difficult at best, assuming we find a compatible donor and find one in a reasonable amount of time. The odds are — well. . .

Wife: *(Puts her hand on the Doctor's, reassuring him.)* I understand. Thank you.

Doctor: *(hesitantly)* Then . . . I'll talk with you later. *(Stands, takes a few steps away, as she and her son, holding each other bow and begin to pray. He turns, shaking his head, not sure any of this is making sense.)*

† † † †

Four young boys are talking: **Rick**, **Andy**, **Vance**, *and* **Adam**.

Rick: We gotta do somethin'.

Andy: Like what?

Rick: I don't know.

Vance: Maybe we could wait for him somewhere, and jump him and all beat him up. I saw that on TV once and it worked good.

Adam: *(brightening)* Yeah! Like outside the gym. He goes there a lot!

Rick: But he's always got his buddies with him. They'd cream us.

Vance: Well . . . we could follow him and figure out somewhere's he's by himself.

Adam: Yeah! *Then* we'll get him!

Andy: Or we could see if he wants to come to the lockin at church Friday.

ALL: *(They all look at him in shock and say simultaneously.)* What ?!? Are you nuts? Not Simpson!

Andy: Well, you said you wanted to get him alone — away from his buddies, right?

Rick: Yeah?

Andy: And you want to gang up on him — all of us there and Simpson by himself.

Vance: But that's so's we can beat him up — not be his friend all of a sudden!

Adam: Yeah! He's been bullyin' us long enough. He deserves it!

Vance: He's got it comin'.

Rick: *(with derision)* You scared, Andy?

Andy: No. But if we beat him up, then he's just gonna keep bullyin' us and nothing will ever change and we'll just keep being scared of him —

Rick: I thought you said you weren't scared.

Andy: I'm not. I'm tired of being scared of Simpson. We don't have to be afraid of him. We gotta do something different!

Vance: *(Thinks he's gotten the idea.)* So we beat him up at the lockin!

Andy: No! We don't beat him up.

Rick: *(to Andy)* Then what do we do to him?

Andy: *We* shoot baskets, skate, watch the movies like we always do and maybe Simpson'll do it, too.

Rick: *(in shock)* With *us*?

Andy: *(timidly — after all it does sound preposterous)* It's possible.

They sit in silence, thinking about this improbability until Vance says . . .

Vance: Awww, he probably won't come anyway.

They are all visibly relieved at this.

Rick: Yeah, he probably won't.

Andy: But he might. You never know.

They all look at him.

Adam: *(angry)* Come on, Andy? This guy's been bullyin' us since second grade and now you want to invite him to *our* church, with us? I don't want to. I don't want to be his friend.

Vance: Yeah, Andy. We don't want to *like* him.

Andy: Then nothin'll ever change.

*Two women are talking: **Judy** and **Kathy***

Judy: I've never seen anything like it, Kath. At first, I thought she was in denial. But she talked so freely about Josh's death. So did Tim.

Kathy: Maybe they went into therapy.

Judy: No. Not Belinda.

Kathy: I don't know how she's even functioning. If that had happened to my four year old, dying so tragically like that — I don't know what would get me first — the guilt or the depression.

Judy: I've never seen her depressed. Quiet, yes. Even withdrawn. But not depressed.

Kathy: Maybe she hasn't really grieved.

Judy: I don't think that's it, either. I saw her the first few weeks and she grieved, believe me. And she went through the anger. But now—now, she has such a peace about it. This calm, even when she talks about Josh with tears in her eyes. She says she knows he's with Jesus and that they'll be together again. And she goes on. It seems very real to her.

Kathy: *(in a very matter-of-fact voice)* Well, everybody has their own way of dealing with things, I guess. Some people use religion.

Judy: *(still puzzled)* Religion? This is not like any religion *I've* ever experienced.

FREEZE

O BEAUTIFUL

by Matt Tullos

A world-hunger emphasis reading

Cast: *Four Readers*

#1: O beautiful for spacious sky,

#2: Everyone wants a piece of the pie.

#3: Our land is dry, our crops are dead,

#4: Our children cry for a crust of bread.

#1: We try to give our children the best.

#2: We work hard for the money,

#1: No time to rest.

#3: Our fields will see no fruited plain.

#4: Through hunger and war, our children are slain.

#3: America! America! God shed His grace on *thee!*

#4: And yet we cry for food and aid, and no one hears our plea.

#1: He crowned *our* good with brotherhood

#2: Yet are we doing all we should from sea to shining sea?

#1: O beautiful for spacious sky,

#2: Everyone wants a piece of the pie.

#3: Our land is dry,

#4: Our crops are dead,

#3 & #4: Our children cry for a crust of bread.

MY LITTLE LAMB

by Christy Doyle

A Mother's Day sketch

Cast: *Mary (mother), Katie (her young daughter)*

Setting: *Mary is on the phone with her sister.*

Mary: Hey, Linda. *(listens)* Well, the same to you. Happy Mother's Day. You must be excited. I remember I was so excited on my first Mother's Day. *(listens)* You bet! He's taking me out to eat. You know Danny, He's treating me like a queen. *(listens)* Well, thank you, you deserve it, too. *(listens)* Yeah, it is kinda sad. It's been three months since Mom died. She always made Mother's Day special. Hey, she made every day special. She always called me her little lamb of God . . . I'm gonna miss that. *(listens)* Katie's doing fine. She's certainly my little lamb of God. She's taking ballet lessons now. Well, how's Pete?*(listens)*The pictures are great. *(listens)* Oh, OK. I love you, I'll see you in June. Bye, bye.

Katie: *(enters carrying two gifts)* Happy Mother's Day, Mommy.

Mary: Thank you, Sweetie. Where's Daddy?

Katie: He's wrapping another present for you.

Mary: Well, should I open this one?

Katie nods her head. They sit on a couch and Mary opens a present. The first is some kind of lamb . . . a picture, figurine, hook rug . . . whatever.

Mary: Where did you get this?

Katie: Daddy got it at Grandma's old house.

Mary: Did you know that Grandma made it when I was a little girl? It used to be in my room when I was younger. Would you like to have it in your room?

Katie: *(nods)*

Mary: *(holding up photo album)* Another present?

Katie: *(nods)*

Mary: For me?

Katie: *(nods)*

Mary: It looks like a photo album. I think maybe it is.

Katie: *(nods)*

Mary: *(opens the photo album)* Oh, these were all Grandma's pictures that she took of me.Oh, Sweetie, your grandma was the best mommy in the whole world.

Katie: No she wasn't.

Mary: What??

Katie: You're the best mommy in the whole world.

Mary: Oh, my little lamb of God. *(She kisses Katie and then looks at the album.)* The last picture Mom has in here is a picture of me—and I'm pregnant with you.

Katie: Happy Mother's Day, Mommy!

THE DIVORCE

by Zack Galloway

Communicating Christ in the midst of tragedy

Cast: *Jay* and *Marci*, *teenage friends*

Jay is in his room packing a suit case.

Marci: Hey Jay!

Jay: Hi.

Marci: I haven't heard from you in a while. How's everything going?

Jay: As well as can be expected under the circumstances.

Marci: Are you going on a trip?

Jay: I guess you could say that. You haven't heard?

Marci: Heard what?

Jay: I'm sorry, Marci. I should have called you earlier.

Marci: What is it? What's going on?

Jay: My parents are planning on getting a divorce.

Marci: You're kidding...

Jay: I wish I was. Mom and Sarah and I are going to have to move in with her parents in Wichita.

Marci: Wichita? Wichita, Kansas?

Jay: You got it.

Marci: I don't know what to say. I'm sorry.

Jay: Me too. You don't know how sorry I am. A month ago everything seemed fine. Sure they had their problems. I always thought everybody did and that everybody got over it. Worked it out. . . But not Mom and Dad. I didn't even know what was happening. They just walked in and calmly told me that the marriage was dead. *(pause)* I know that it happens everywhere, all the time. But I didn't expect it to happen to us. Did you hear what I just said? *"Us."* Who are *we* now? *We* aren't a family anymore. It's Mom and Dad, and then Sarah and I are kind of in this gray area. Not belonging to either one.

Marci: How is Sarah doing?

Jay: She's too young to really understand. All she knows is that it hurts. *(angrily)* I feel so numb. It's like I don't care anymore. I guess life is that way.

Marci: It shouldn't be.

Jay: But it is.

They hug.

Jay: I'm going to miss you. You've always been there for me when I've had problems. You're like a big sister.

Marci: I wish there was some way we could put the pieces back together again, but only your parents can do that.

Jay: Marci, there's something different about you. You've got something that none of my other friends seem to have. You seem so at peace with yourself. I know you have problems too. How are we supposed to cope with things like this?

Marci: *(long pause)* It's, well, it's my faith. That's how I make it.

Jay: I've been to church before, and . . .

Marci: I'm not talking about church. I'm talking about a relationship with Jesus Christ. I was as lost as any person could be before I asked Jesus to take control of my life. It was like I was on a journey without a map.

Jay: That's me. That's where I am. I don't know where I'm going with my life or what I'm doing.

Marci: You need a guide. You need Jesus.

ORGANIZATION OF MINISTRY

by Pamela Baker

All are necessary parts of the body

Cast: *Mr. Hart, Ms. Foote, Mr. Hand, Ms. Palmer, Iris*

Mr. Hart brings in an easel with an organization chart on it. The chart looks like a stick figure. As each candidate steps over to the workroom side of the stage where there is a table and a few chairs set up, the corresponding body part will be drawn or pasted on the chart.

Mr. Hart: This is going to be the best ministry in the association. — the best outreach program ever. I'm interviewing top-notch people with very diverse skills. I'm sure I'll be able to put together a first-rate team. We're going to reach millions of people with the good news that we'll be distributing. Here is my first candidate now.

Ms. Foote: Hello, I'm Fleeta Foote. I can carry good news faster and farther than anyone. I've won several speed-walking competitions,10 k's, and I completed a 20-mile walkathon just last week.

Mr. Hart: Those are very good qualifications, we can certainly use your talents. You will be in charge of deliveries. Please step over here. *(Ms. Foote steps to the workroom and starts pacing. Both feet go on chart.)* Ah! and here's my next applicant.

Mr. Hand: Hi, I'm Bill Hand. I have the best handwriting in the area. I've studied calligraphy. I'm also very fast at addressing envelopes. Good handwriting makes a much better impression than typewriting on the outside of an envelope anyway.

Mr. Hart: Fine, fine. We'll get you to work addressing envelopes right away. *(Steps over and sits at the desk but can't start because there is no mailing list. One hand goes on the chart.)*

Ms. Palmer: Hello, Mr. Hart. I'm Shirley Palmer. I think I can be a big help to you. I have the best typing skills around. I can type 80 words a minute. I could type up the tracts and compile the mailing list.

Mr. Hart: That's great, get started right away.

Ms. Palmer: OK. *(Walks to office and starts typing. Other hand goes on chart).*

Mr. Hart: I can't believe how well everything is going so far. My organization chart is complete and I have an excellent staff. *(Sits down in a relaxed posture.)*

Meanwhile in the office, the mailing list is getting written and envelopes are getting addressed, but there is nothing to deliver and Ms. Foote is getting impatient. She walks back and sees Mr. Hart resting.

Ms. Foote: Mr. Hart, I don't think this is working out very well. I think I should go home. I don't have anything to do.

Mr. Hart: But you can't go home now. You are very important. You are the feet that carry the good news.

Ms. Foote: That's the point. There's nothing to carry.

Mr. Hart: Hold on a minute while I figure out

66

the problem. *(looking at chart)* My chart is complete. You all are supposedly very competent. I don't understand. Why can't you do a simple task.

Ms. Palmer and ***Mr. Hand*** come back over.

Ms. Palmer: Mr. Hart, your mailing list is finished.

Mr. Hand: All the envelopes are addressed also. I'm taking off.

Ms. Foote: Good I can start delivering. *(Starts for office.)*

Ms. Palmer: There is nothing else for me to type so I guess I'll be going, too. Bye.

Mr. Hart: You couldn't be finished already.

Ms. Foote: *(coming back with some addressed empty envelopes)* Mr. Hart I can't deliver these. They're empty.

Mr. Hart: Wait, everyone, you can't go yet. What happened? Why is there nothing in the envelopes?

Ms. Palmer: That wasn't our responsibility.

Mr. Hand: We did our jobs.

Ms. Foote: I would have, but I didn't have a job to do.

Mr. Hart: I don't understand this whole mess. My chart . . . it was complete. I was so organized. What happened?

Iris: Mr. Hart, I'm Iris. *(tugs on his sleeve)* Excuse me, sir.

Mr. Hart: Please don't bother me; I have a crisis to solve right now.

Iris: *(Points to the chart, but **Mr. Hart** doesn't notice.)* Why is the head missing?

Mr. Hart: My head is right here. What are you talking about? What are you doing here anyway?

Iris: I heard you say the chart is complete, but it's not. The head is missing.

Mr. Hart: *(Takes a long look at the chart.)* You know you're right. Without the head we had no communication or direction.

Mr. Hand: We were each doing our own job.

Ms. Palmer: Or what we thought was our job,

Mr. Hand: But without working together, without unity of purpose, we couldn't get anything done.

Ms. Foote: I see, we need someone to coordinate our efforts. Someone in charge who can point us all in the same direction.

Iris: Yes, but it's more than that. We need a specific head. One who can focus our efforts for His purpose. Ephesians 5:23b says: ". . . Christ is the head of the church, his body, of which he is the Savior" *(NIV).* — and 1 Corinthians 12:12 says: "The body is a unit, though it is made up of many parts; and though all its parts are many, they form one body. So it is with Christ" *(NIV).*

Mr. Hart: I really blew it, didn't I? I was so sure that if I assembled people with the different skills required, everything would work out.

Iris: You were on the right track. We do need to use our different skills. However, we need to realize that others are as important, and to coordinate our actions to suit *His* purpose.

Mr. Hart: *(Walks to the chart, places the head at the top, and places a cross inside it.)* I guess I learned my lesson. Now do you think we can finish this task?

Iris: *(Places a heart on the chart.)* Of course, now that your heart is in the right place.

THE WITNESS

by Pamela Baker

Simple truth: the remedy in complex times

Cast: *Marie (business woman); Cleaner*

*Spotlight comes on. A young woman, **Marie**, is sitting at a desk which is laden with papers. There are some rolled-up drawings on the side and an old jacket and hard hat hidden from view. The rest of the stage should be dark.*

***Marie** is dressed in a suit. She is struggling with the paper work trying hard to concentrate. **Marie**'s prerecorded thoughts are played while she reacts, sometimes looking around as if she is making sure no one is watching. Lines in all capitals are* **spoken aloud** *to unseen colleagues and will have to be timed with the "thoughts."*

Start tape.

Marie: I've been here six months, and haven't done anything interesting yet . . . or challenging, other than keeping my mind on my job. I can't seem to concentrate for more than 10 minutes at a time. This is not what I expected when I was in college. Funny, everyone back home thinks my life is so great. I have a college degree and a career. They think I have my act together.

OH, GEORGE, DID YOU GET THAT MEMO I SENT ABOUT THE MATERIAL I NEED? YES, I NEED IT BY FRIDAY OR I'LL MISS MY DEADLINE. . . .

speaking of deadlines, this report is due —

UH, HI MR SIMMONS

— right now!

I'M SORRY. I'LL HAVE IT ON YOUR DESK FIRST THING TOMORROW MORNING.

Great, Marie, if you could just concentrate you would already have this stupid thing done. *(goes back to the report for a second)* Is this all there is? This report is so ridiculous. It's not going to serve any purpose other than keeping me busy. My other projects aren't much better. Right now this job is all I have. I haven't made any friends, other than work acquaintances. I've even tried meeting people in laundromats and grocery stores. I feel so alone.

Why do I even bother to get up in the morning. I don't have a goal or a purpose anymore. I just feel so lost. I didn't have this problem when I was in college, my purpose in life was to graduate! Well, I graduated and got a decent job; now what?

Stop tape.

WHAT! WE HAVE TO GO TO THE SITE RIGHT NOW?! GIVE ME A MINUTES.

She gathers drawings, picks up the jacket and hard hat, and runs off.

Spot fades off, then back on.

Walks back to the desk.

GOOD NIGHT, JOE. NO, I HAVE TO FINISH THIS REPORT. I TOLD SIMMONS I'D GET IT TO HIM FIRST THING TOMORROW. YEAH, SEE YA TOMORROW. *(Sits down, starts getting organized.)*

Start tape.

We rushed off to the site for nothing! I could have solved that problem over the phone. My boss gets spun out over the smallest things. Now everyone is gone and I have to stay and finish this *(self-censored)* report. Will this day ever end? Does it matter? It's not like there's anyone waiting for me at home anyway.

Stop tape.

Cleaner *enters unseen, though he or she is heard singing a hymn.*

Marie: *(looks up annoyed)* WHO IS SINGING? *(gets more aggravated, gets up to investigate. Spot follows her.)* WOULD YOU PLEASE STOP THAT RACKET, I CAN'T CONCEN. . .

Cleaner *and* **Marie** *are both in the spotlight.* **Marie** *pauses for a moment then goes back to the desk.* **Cleaner** *pauses briefly, not sure whether she heard anything and not seeing anyone goes back to singing. Spot follows* **Marie** *back to desk.* **Marie's** *remaining lines can either be on the tape or spoken but it is very important that the following dialogue and the cleaning person's songs be well-timed. A line or two of each song should be heard clearly before the dialogue is spoken and then should be sung or hummed softly during the speech.*

Marie: I wonder what she has to sing about. I wouldn't want that job. I couldn't afford it.

Cleaner: *(Sings "Closer than a Brother," by Eddie Smith from* Sing Now *by Otis Skillings, 1975, Lillenas Publishing.)*

Marie: She probably has a really close family. I miss mine. Maybe I should call my brother tonight. He always knows how to lift my spirits . . . I have a lot going for me. Why am I so miserable?

Cleaner: *(Sings "The Church's One Foundation," #350,* The Baptist Hymnal, *1991.)*

Marie: I tried going to church to make some friends. I just got depressed. Everyone was there with their families, spouses. I was the only single person there. Nobody really tried to get to know me. No, that's not for me right now. I can still believe in God without going to church.

What I need is a new goal. Maybe grad school. I might be able to make some closer friends there. I never had any problem making friends in college. I wish I was still there.

I don't seem to have any direction or purpose. What I really need is to know what this is all for. What is the reason for living, what is my reason for being here?

Cleaner: *(hums or sings softly)* "I Love to Tell the Story"(#572), or "On Jordan's Stormy Banks" (#521), or "'Tis So Sweet to Trust in Jesus" (#411) (*The Baptist Hymnal*,1991).

Marie: *(listens, mood is softening)* What does she have that I don't have?

Cleaner: *(loudly)* "Jesus, Jesus, precious Jesus."

Marie: *(Freezes for a moment, gets up, and starts walking toward* **Cleaner**.*)* Hey, can I talk to you?

DADDY

by Leigh Ann Thomas

Great for Father's Day!

Cast: *Child 1, Child 2, Teenager 1, Teenager 2, Woman 1, Woman 2*

You may use only two actors to portray the children and the teens, heightening the transition from loving youngsters to defiant youths. Children hold a doll or other toy, teenagers smack on gum.

Child 1: Do you know my daddy? Well, if you don't, you ought to! He's the most wonderful daddy in the world! And strong too! He can pick me up and swing me around—so you'd better watch out, 'cause if you pick on me, my daddy's gonna. . .

Child 2: . . . beat you up—'cause he's big and strong. Yeah, you'd better not mess with my daddy!

Child 1: And he's smart too! He went to school for years and years. He knows all the answers to all the questions. . . like. . .

Child 2: What are clouds made of?

Child 1: How do airplanes stay up in the sky?

Child 2: Where do snowflakes come from?

Child 1: And Daddy's fun too! He takes me fishin' and swimmin' and he teaches me things too, like. . .

Child 2: . . . how to ride my bike, and. . .

Child 1: . . . how to play ball. . .

Child 2: . . . and how to love Jesus.

Children exit as Teenagers enter.

Teen 1: Dad's about to drive me crazy!

Teen 2: There's always one more chore to do. . . "Take out the trash; mow the lawn; watch your little sister."

Teen 1: "Do this, do that". . . there's never time for anything I want to do.

Teen 1: And if we dare complain, what do we hear?

Both teens: "When I was a boy. . ."

Teen 1: "I had to walk five miles to school . . .

Teen 2: uphill. . .

Both teens : in the snow!"

Teen 1: And if I hear "money doesn't grow on trees, you know" one more time, I think I'll scream!

Teen 2: He just doesn't know what it's like to be a teenager.

Teen 1: Yeah, he just doesn't get it!

Teenagers exit and **Women** *enter.* **Women** *speak out to audience.*

Woman 1: Daddy, remember those early years, when you could do no wrong in my eyes? You were my first love, you know.

Woman 2: And oh, how hard my teenage years must have been for you — with me constantly challenging everything you said.

Woman 1: But I look at you differently now, Daddy — not with the eyes of a child — for over the years I began to see that maybe you weren't the strongest or the smartest.

Woman 2: And not with the eyes of a teenager, always probing and challenging. But I see you through the eyes of an adult now, Daddy, full of love and precious memories of my growing-up years.

Woman 1: And there've been some changes — your hair, once dark and wavy, is now a fine, silvery gray, and your eyes are now surrounded by little lines, permanently engraved from the years of joy and pain.

Woman 2: I remember those eyes, Daddy — darkening with anger at my rebellion or twinkling with laughter at my childish pranks — your wonderful eyes that quietly sought and expected the best from me.

Woman 1: And, Daddy, your hands, now a little worn, that could be so loving whether in a gentle caress, or while holding the rod of discipline.

Woman 2: Your hands, that worked so hard to provide for a family — that cut the grass, took out trash, and put toys together on Christmas Eve.

Woman 1: Hands that removed splinters from tiny fingers, applied first aid, and wiped away my tears.

Woman 2: Hands that held the family Bible during devotions, and made sure your family was in church on Sunday. Hands that once cradled me and now cradle my children.

Woman 1: I look to you, Dad, you who for years I've know as father, provider, protector, and my vision that seemed so blurred through my teenage years, slowly begins to clear. And I see, for maybe the first time, that God gave you to me as an example of Himself. And that through you I have been given a glimpse of the wondrous love of my Creator.

Woman 2: And, Daddy, I know you won't always be with me, but you are giving me a legacy of Christian love to share with my children.

Woman 1: For now I see that the greatest gift of lasting value that you have given me is not one of worldly wealth, for that passes away, but it's a life lived to the glory of God. For the effects of such a life, Daddy, reach far into eternity. Thank you. I love you.

IS JESUS STILL HERE?

by Wanda Pearce

Choose this spontaneous piece to make your Christmas worship meaningful

Excuse me for interrupting . . . but I need to ask some Christmas questions.

When I was little, I went to church with my parents, most every Sunday. They taught me that I would meet God there, and some day, when I was old enough, I would know Jesus as my Savior.

I met God there and saw Him in the kindness of the people — the way they loved and encouraged each other. And because of their love for me, I came to know Jesus, and accepted Him as my personal Savior.

As I grew older, I learned that He lived in me. He taught me to care about others and to do what was right. My moral values were formed with the help of my parents and the church folks. I hope you have had a similar experience.

But back to my questions this Christmas. Is Jesus still here? Can we find Him in the caring and sacrificial giving to persons with deep pain and needs? Is He still working in this world of no visual peace? Do we still see Him in Christians who love one another? Or have we forgotten that youth and children and the world need to see Him in us? Are we so busy with our own agenda we have neglected to show Him to our world? Is this the reason for the hopelessness, drugs, family problems, teen pregnancies, and mindless violence?

Tell me this Christmas, is Jesus still here?

MARY

by Leigh Ann Thomas

Before the birth of Jesus

Setting: *Mary, "great with child," is packing for her upcoming trip to Bethlehem. She is very busy until she is interrupted by a "kick" from baby Jesus.*

There! I hope that's everything. Mother told me to pack light, but it's so hard to know what to take and what to leave. Oh! . . . *(feeling baby kick)* I'll definitely be taking *you*, little one — don't you worry about that! I can't believe how big you're getting. I can't believe how big *I'm* getting. *(smiling)*

(more to herself) It seems like only yesterday that I was just a child — and now — *I* have a child within me. Oh, little one — what a scene you are making. Not everyone understands, you know. Mother and Father are trying to, but I think most people don't understand why Joseph didn't just. . . Joseph, oh my Joseph — how wonderful he's been — and after what he's been through! I'll never forget his face when I told him about you. There were so many emotions — shock, anger, hurt — and that look of betrayal. Oh the thought of how he must have suffered pierces my very soul.

But it's all right now — the angel explained everything. It's so good to know that Joseph believes — so good. *(feeling baby kick again)* My goodness, you're moving a lot today.

We have quite a journey ahead of us, you know. Can you believe it? All the way to Bethlehem! Mother and Father have doubts about me going when your birth is so near, but Joseph and I know that this is right. That this is how the Father wants it.

Oh little one, I feel so many things — excitement, joy — fear, uncertainty. My life has changed so much in such a short time. The angel said that I was highly favored — but sometimes I wonder. How could anyone be worthy of such a calling? Maybe — maybe when I hold you, when I see you — I'll understand things a little better. And oh how I long to hold you. To touch your sweet face to mine — to feel your tiny fingers in my hand. Oh, my son — will people know who you are? Will they really understand?

I don't know what lies ahead — but I know that I love you. And I love the Father who gave you to me. *(pausing, deep in thought)*

(realizing she has things to do) Look at us, just sitting here when there's so much to be done! Oh, I hear Joseph now. *(calling to him)* I'm coming Joseph, I'm coming!

She exits.

MARY

by Leigh Ann Thomas

After the Birth

Shhhh. It's all right—quiet down now, Mother's here. That's better. Let's try to rest for awhile, Little One. Or should I say— Jesus? *(smiling)* Oh how I love the sound of Your name. Jesus, my Jesus.

I can't believe you're finally here! You're more wonderful than I ever imagined. *(smiling)* I see You looking at me — You like to hear Mother's voice, don't you? *(cuddles, stroking baby)* What is going on behind those expressive little eyes? *(sighing)* Oh, if I only knew what the Father had planned for your life. Will you know joy? Will you know pain? I pray that you will always know of my love for you. *(pausing and smiling)* How can someone so small have such a hold on my heart?

This day has been so overwhelming! You have had so many visitors. *(laughing)* Not that *you'll* remember, little sleepy head. The shepherds seemed in awe of you and they whispered about so many wonderful things the angels had told them. They actually came to the city to find you—and to worship you! Oh my son — the words I heard today I will forever treasure in my heart. *(**Mary** holds **Jesus** close then lays Him in the manger.)*

(She looks heavenward.) Oh Father, does Bethlehem realize what has happened here in her midst? Is it possible that some will never understand Your great love for them? *(pausing, looking at **Jesus**)* I pray for wisdom, Father, and for strength to be the mother You would have me to be. I know, Father, that the time will come when Joseph and I must share this precious gift with the world. But for now, I thank You — and I praise You for our little Jesus — our precious Jesus. *(leaning over to kiss **Jesus**)* Good night, my son.

CHRISTMAS PROMISE

by bonnie benham*

Great Christmas Reminder for the Promise Keeper

Cast:
Mary: Vulnerable, soft, Christian woman at wit's end in marriage
Ted: Business oriented, hard worker, newly learning more about the Lord and his wife
Announcer: Offstage voice (may be on tape if preferred)

Setting: *The setting is **Mary** and **Ted**'s home three days before Christmas.*
There is an air of depression, yet hope with Mary. Ted's attitude is one of frustration.
As the drama ends, the marriage has a new start in the right direction with both happy, hopeful,
and content. Christ has become the center, the promises — the stepping stones.

Props: *Decorated holiday tree stage center with four unwrapped gifts, holiday gift bags, and tissue.*
*Make sure there is ample room for **Mary** to crawl all the way around (under) the tree.*
Telephone on small phone table down stage front center.
Simple small kitchen table and chairs (two) stage right.
Simple chair stage left with folders and papers as possible bedroom
where Ted goes after yelling "Good heavens, doesn't he know it's Christmas!"
On kitchen table there is a radio, a teapot, a cup and saucer, and a casserole dish.

Lights up as holiday music begins. A few bars of each of the following (or pieces of your choice) — secular or religious: "Jingle Bells," "Hark the Herald Angels Sing," "Home for the Holidays."

Announcer: *(offstage or recorded)* Two shopping days till Christmas, folks!

Mary: *(turns radio off, counting money)* $145, $146, $147, $148 — I just don't have it. I'll have to wait till *next* Christmas to afford it. If Ted would stay home Tuesday night, I could get some overtime in — maybe then I could . . . No, he rarely gets a night out, and, I did say it was fine with me. I even told him it would be good for him!

Who am I kidding, I need him *here*!!!! I wonder if he has a gift for me? *(looking under tree for her gift from **Ted**, big scramble all the way around on all fours, flat on tummy, stretching, ending up head first on all fours coming from behind the tree and facing congregation with a big disappointed expression as **Ted** enters)*

Ted: *(not seeing **Mary** at first)* You mean the gifts aren't wrapped yet? Mary, what've you been doing? We're supposed to be at Mother's by 8:00 p.m. You know she's planned a big gathering and *she* doesn't like to be kept waiting. *(sighting Mary and doing a double take)* Mary, what *are* you doing?

75

Mary: The casserole's waiting, and, it won't take me five minutes with the gifts. I know it's hard on her . . . It's just . . .

Ted: *(very exasperated)* What?

Mary: I'll wrap the gifts.

Ted: *(smiles)*

Mary: *(humming sadly while wrapping gifts)*

Ted: *(Heads for phone, dials quickly, muffles mouth.)* I goofed. I know it. I don't know it. Well, I . . . *(mumbles indistinguishably)* . . . Oh! Okay. Okay. Yes. Alright. Thanks, Buddy. *(hangs up)*

Mary: *(Stands holding packages giving hard-to-come-by smile.)* Ready?

Ted: Oh, *(Grabs casserole from kitchen table and comes back to Mary.)* Yes. *(clears throat)* Ready! *(Couple leaves stage right.)*

Blackout. Brief Christmas song (few bars) plays. Lights up as couple reenters kitchen, laughing.

Mary: *(sets casserole on kitchen table)* Oh no. You've got to be kidding. Did he see you laughing?

Ted: Who knows? *(big smile)* All I know is when his head came up from the plate with whipped cream covering his mustache, he looked like a polar walrus. And then, *(laughing so hard he can hardly talk)* when he innocently gave his whole speech like that, I could hardly contain myself. *(The telephone rings, and, Mary heads for it. Ted walks to the bedroom shaking his head with a big smile, until he sees a folder of work papers, then, he gets a serious, stern attitude.)*

Mary: *(answering phone)* Oh, Mom, did I forget something? Yes, I know there were a lot of people there. Thank you for all you did. I *(is cut off and gives expression as though she's experienced this a million times before—pause—big smile)* Oh, Mom. You will! Well, how did you find . . . ? *(nods head yes)* Mother told you. Well, yes. Ted really needs one, and, I've been trying so hard to save money for it, but . . . I . . . Thank you, Mom. Well, yes. I'll get you paid back with my next check. By then, Ted will know, so, it won't matter. I'm so excited! Ted'll really be surprised. Yes, Mom. I love you, too. Good night. *(pause)* Ted . . . honeyeeeeeee!

Ted: *(sternly yelling from bedroom)* What now Mary? You know I've got to get this presentation together for tomorrow. I don't know who Mr. Brown thinks I am. I put eight hours in at the office and bring home nine hours worth of preparation. I told him this client is pushing too far, paying too little, and wanting deadlines that are totally impossible — especially at Christmas. Good heavens, doesn't he *know* it's Christmas! *(Throws his hands up in the air and back down while he is doing paper work, with majorfrustration.)*

Mary: *(Who has stood frozen with big eyes by phone during Ted's entire monologue, crosses sadly to kitchen. She pours tea from pot on kitchen table as though her balloon has totally burst. She sits.)* Lord, so many years I've prayed for him—so many years I've tried to witness. Thank You, Lord, for this day and *Your* love. You alone see me through. Thank You for a way to get Ted the new briefcase. The special gadgets in it will make his work easier out of the office. Thank You too, Lord, that Mom asked me some questions about You tonight at the dinner. Thank You for all my loved ones, Lord. *(pause)* I need to be honest with you though. You know what I'm feeling in my heart anyway. *(Ted appears at door.)* You see, I've felt very alone in this marriage, and, I'm at the end of my rope. If Ted can't find time for me now, what will he do when — well if — a baby comes? Will there be time then? And, what about Sundays? Why does he always need to sleep in? I've done all I know to do — all I know You want me to do. I give up. I give it to you. Whatever you decide, I will do, Lord. Just tell me — Your will. Not mine.

Ted: *(who has been going through several emotions while watching and listening to her, softly says)* Bah, humbug.

Mary: *(not understanding the words but loving the new tone, looks up smiling hopefully)* What?

Ted: I said I've been a bah humbug. *(He holds his hand out to he r— she comes to him. He puts her hand in his, kisses it, and leads her to the Christmas tree.)* It's early, and, I know I haven't done well. . . *(Reaches to treetop for envelope on very top tip of tree with big gold star on it while she looks as though — that's where it was!)* but, I want you to know, I love you . . . and, I've been trying to "clear the decks" early so I could give you a special Christmas this year. I see I've disappointed you as usual. I want you to know, I didn't mean to. I *never* mean to. *(Hands her the envelope.)* I've been going to some new men's meetings at church, and, I've been learning a lot about. . . *(pause)* Mary, I have no box this Christmas — no bow, no pretty wrapping, but I. . . *(He gingerly takes envelope from **Mary** who has been standing there totally stunned and visibly moved. **Ted** opens the envelope, glances at **Mary** with definite love in his eyes, and begins reading the Promise Keepers' seven promises.)*

I AM COMMITTED TO:**

1. *Honor Jesus Christ through prayer, worship, and obedience to His Word in the power of the Holy Spirit;*

2. *Pursue vital relationships with a few other men, understanding that I need brothers to help me keep my promises;*

3. *Spiritual, moral, ethical, and sexual purity;*

4. *Build strong marriages and families through love, protection, and biblical values;*

5. *Support the mission of my church, by honoring and praying for my pastor and by actively giving my time and resources;*

6. *Reach beyond any racial and denominational barriers to understand the power of biblical unity;*

7. *Influence my world, being obedient to the Great Commandment (Mark 12:30-31) and the Great Commission (Matthew 28:19-20).*

Mary: *(totally speechless)* This is the best Christmas ever. Sorta like God's gift to us through Christ — love, mercy, forgiveness, gentleness, kindness, tenderness.

*They hug while turning in circles, with **Mary's** face ending up towards the audience. **Ted's** back is to audience. **Mary** mouths a big thank you to the heavens.*

Blackout. A Christmas hymn plays for a few bars to finalize the ending.

---

* bonnie prefers that her name be lower-cased. It is her artist's signature and a reminder to her and a witness to others of her humbleness in the gift given, knowing the talent is a gift on loan from God.

**These are the seven promises of the Promise Keepers organization, P.O. Box 18376, Boulder Colorado, 80308. Phone: (303) 421-2800.

COMPARING LISTS

by bonnie benham*

Christmas Feature that compares materialism and true generosity

Purpose: *To show the audience how our prayers sometimes sound like Santa Claus lists, and to help them better understand, through seeing themselves, how to pray.*

Cast:
Little Girl
Youth: *Casual, contemporary, today, male*
Man: *Late thirties, early forties*
Older Lady: *Wholesome*
Santa Claus

Props: *1 chair for **Santa** and 1 chair for **Older Lady**.*

*Spot up on **Little Girl**. Only she actually goes to Santa. The rest have individual marks on the stage. Pace quickens and builds, then slows with lady.*

Little Girl: *(sitting on Santa's lap, demanding)* I want a dolly like Jill's and some of those neat tennis shoes that light up.

*Spot off. Spot up on **Youth**.*

Youth: *(pleading — looks up to God)* Lord, all the girls think I'm a nerd. If Beth would only go out with me Saturday night. Please, Lord, let Beth say she'll go.

*Spot off. Spot up on **Little Girl**.*

Little Girl: Susie has three of them. I want three too. And, new jeans and a cartoon character shirt. Oh, and . . .

*Spot goes directly to **Youth**.*

Youth: *(cutting her off)* Why do I get so tongue tied? They tell us in church "True Love Waits." Lord, I think I'll be waiting when I'm 80 years old.

*Spot goes directly to **Little Girl**.*

Little Girl: I need money to buy Mommy and Daddy a present.

*Spot widens to include **Youth**.*

Youth: A car. If I had a car, maybe she'd go.

Little Girl: A teddy bear.

*Spot widens to include **Man**.*

Man: *(depressed)* Father, I pray and pray — a bigger check — a new job. I can't feed my family on this. *(Shows empty pockets.)*

Youth: A *red* car. Oh yeah . . . thanks.

Man: An understanding wife. Janet nags me to no end.

*Spot narrows again and moves to **Older Lady**.*

Older Lady: *(joyful, real — on knees, elbows on chair, in prayer)* I praise You for Your mercy, for Your forgiveness and for Your gracious ways. We got through today, Lord. I couldn't have done it without You. You are so faithful. I could start no day without You. Thank You, Lord, for the way You worked out Kendra's problems. Please be with Cathy and little Moody and continue their healing. May they see Your ways and learn to trust and love You. Bless our pastor and his little family. I know he feels alone at times and needs Your love through some of us. Show me today what You'd have me do. And, last, how can I ever close without an overflowing heart for James. Fifty-five years together and we know it's *You*! We thank You, who showed us each step of the way. *(smiles)* I praise You now and forever. I ask these things knowing You know best, Lord. In Christ's name, amen.

Spot slowly closes off. All characters leave pulpit. Lights up for sermon.

* bonnie prefers that her name be lower-cased. It is her artist's signature and a reminder to her and a witness to others of her humbleness in the gift given, knowing the talent is a gift on loan from God.

HELLO

by Tim Shamburger
Divine intervention through a phone call

Ralph and Will are on opposite sides of the stage.

Will: *(on the phone)* No, Ma'am, I'm not trying to be annoying, I'm sorry, Ma'am. *(Hangs up.)* I hate this job. Lord, I don't know why I was in a hit and run, but I still put my faith in You. I sure don't know why I'm in a wheelchair, but I still trust You. What I really don't understand is why the only job I can get is phone sales for a long distance company. God, give me strength.

Ralph: God, if You are up there, help me!

The phone rings.

Ralph: Hello.

Will: Hello, my name is Will, and I would like to offer you an opportunity to save plenty on your long distance calls. Here at CDI Telecommunications, we feel it is important to work with folks to reduce the amount you spend on calls each month. Do you make regular calls to relatives?

Ralph: No, my parents passed away when I was young, I really don't have any . . .

Will: Do you make long distance calls to friends from college?

Ralph: I couldn't afford college. I really don't have any friends. I really don't need this . . .

Will: Well, at CDI we are interested in you saving money so much that we are willing to give you $10 worth of free calls, just for switching to us.

Ralph: I really don't think you understand, it won't matter what my phone bill is tomorrow. I'm going to kill myself.

Will: *(silent for a moment)* I see.

Ralph: I can't believe it, I finally found the perfect comeback for a phone salesman. He's speechless.

Will: Look, suicide is no laughing matter.

Ralph: I'm not joking.

Will: I don't know your situation, but, I've wanted to kill myself before . . .

Ralph: Oh, really, I guess you failed. Well, I won't.

Will: I almost succeeded, but God intervened.

Ralph: God? Really, come on.

Will: Really. I was about to kill myself, and I cried out to God for help, and the phone rang. It was a wrong number. The guy on the other end was a Christian. He saved my life.

Ralph: I don't want to hear it . . . just leave me alone. *(starts to hang up.)* No. Wait. Are you still there? Don't hang up. Please. . . help me.

Will: I'm still here. Let me tell you what God has done for me.

EVERYBODY'S DOIN' IT

by David A. Guerrero

A comical sketch that would be a great opening sketch for a "True Love Waits" Rally.

Cast: *Ron* and *Cheryl*, *teenagers*

Setting: *Ron* and *Cheryl* *sit center stage.* ***Ron*** *acts as if he is driving a car.*

Props: *Two chairs*

Ron: *(Brings the car to a stop and parks.)* Well, here we are, alone at last. *(Looks around.)* This spot's perfect.

Cheryl: *(sarcastically)* It had better be perfect. We've been searching for this spot for *(looking at watch.)* a good hour and a half.

Ron: I've been looking forward to this night all week.

Cheryl: *(irritated)* I know, I can tell by the way you've been *(wiping her arm)* drooling on my arm.

Ron: Ah, it's a clear night, a full moon, and you're alone with me. Who knows what could happen? *(Stretches and puts his arm around her.)*

Cheryl: From the look of things I think I'd be better off with the plague.

Ron: *(getting closer to **Cheryl**)* Hey come on, Babe, lets have some fun.

Cheryl: *(Pushes **Ron** back.)* Fun, come on, give me a break. (**Ron** comes back closer.) We're in the middle of nowhere, I can hardly see a thing, and it's so hot in here, *(wiping her shoulder)* something's dripping on me.

Ron: *(Moves back a little and wipes his forehead.)* Oh, that's me. *(Smiles sheepishly and laughs a little.)* Sorry.

Cheryl: *(angrily)* Roll down the windows. *(Rolls her window down and folds her arms in disgust.)*

Ron: *(Rolls down his window.)* Don't worry about a thing. This is going to be a night *(putting his arm around her and pulling her close)* you will never forget.

Cheryl: *(pushing him back and fanning the air)* Back off, this is a date, not a honeymoon.

Ron: Hey, what's the big deal? Everybody's doing it.

Cheryl: Everybody's doing it? Now that's an intelligent reason for doing something — everybody's doing it! I can see it tomorrow. I walk into school and the first person I see says, "Hi Cheryl, the whole school's decided to start *(hitting the side of her head)* hitting themselves in the head. *(Ron looks away a little embarrassed.)* Why don't you try it? Everybody's doing it." *(Cheryl looks away in disgust.)*

Ron: *(more determined)* Cheryl, look, don't worry about it. No one will know.

Cheryl: Yea, right, and you don't have the FBI for parents. I tried to sneak out of the house once, but my mom was waiting for me at the bottom of the stairs. I told her I just wanted to walk around the block, but she knew exactly what I was doing. She said *(talking like a mother might scold her child)* "You're lying to me. I see it written all over your face." Look at my face, *(leaning into Ron)* do you see anything written on my face? No, but she did! Plus, what about God! You're a Christian, aren't you?! Are you dumb enough to think that we could sneak around and fool Him?

Ron looks up and away in disappointment. Cheryl folds her arms and looks away.

Ron: *(apologetically)* Okay, okay, I'm sorry. *(thinking about what he can say to get through to her)* Cheryl, look, I know this is only our *(looking away to think for a moment)* — second date — but, I love you. *(He moves in again.)*

Cheryl: Do you love me more than all the other things you said you loved? *(Ron nods.)* Pizza? Football? Your car? Do you love me more than you love your car?

Ron: *(looking up thoughtfully)* Well . . .

Cheryl: *(shoving Ron)* I'm worth more than that.

Ron: Come on, Cheryl, more than my car?!

Cheryl: *(to self)* I can't believe this guy! Listen, Mr. Testosterone, true love means that you save yourself for the one person you intend to live with for the rest of your life. True love waits for the day you get married and you don't have to go to the great outdoors to do something you might be ashamed of later.

Ron: What's the big deal? It's only love.

Cheryl: *(Cheryl pushes Ron away.)* Wrong again, it's my life. *(Cheryl gets out of car and starts to walk offstage.)* I'm walking home.

Ron: Cheryl, wait! It's dangerous out there!

Cheryl: *(as she walks offstage)* It's safer out here than it is in there!

Ron: Girls. . .why do they have to be so. . . smart.

QUESTIONS

by Tim Logan

Cast: *Angel, Shirley, George,* and *Ida* (*Actors should be in the 30 to 40 year-old range, if possible. If not, some adjustment in the dialogue concerning age may be necessary.*)

Setting: *In heaven. Only a bare stage with three chairs is required. Lighting should be limited to center stage, until the end, when a strong, bright stage light or a very bright spotlight is required.*

*Angel directs **Shirley** to a seat on stage, where **Ida** and **George** are already seated.*

Angel: Right this way, please. Have a seat here until we are ready for you.

Shirley: How long will that be?

Angel: Not long, I assure you. The Most High is nearly finished with the previous group. *(Angel exits.)*

Shirley: Oh, I just can't wait. I have so many things to ask Him.

George: Me too! This is what I've waited for all my life!

Shirley: How long have you been here?

George: I'm not sure. You don't really notice time here, it seems.

Ida: Hello, I'm Ida. Welcome to Heaven.

Shirley: Oh! It gives me goose bumps to hear you say that! Oh, I'm Shirley. *(They shake.hands.)*

George: George. Hi. *(He extends his hand.)*

Ida: *(to Shirley)* Natural causes?

Shirley: Well, it depends on what you call "natural." I'm beginning to see things differently already. They said it was cancer, but it doesn't seem so different from anything else, now. You?

Ida: Car accident. But you're right. It doesn't really matter now, does it? *(Shirley turns to George.)*

George: Me? Just plain old age, I guess.

Shirley: But you don't look more than 35!

George: Great, isn't it? I was 87!

Ida: That's heaven, for you! I was 54, myself!

Shirley: Think of it. We're going to meet God, Himself. I have so many questions.

Ida: Oh, me too! I want to know why there was so much suffering on earth.

George: … and why He couldn't stop all those wars and famines.

Ida: … all the hurricanes and earthquakes!

Shirley: Well, my questions are more personal, like, why did He take my father at such an early age? I was only five. I remember my mother told me to ask God that when I got there. Well, now I'm here. Oh, do you think I'll see my father soon?

George: Probably. My wife should be waiting for me somewhere around here, too, I hope. She always said she wanted to ask God why we couldn't have children.

Ida: I'll tell you what I want to know. Just why did He let Hitler do what he did to all those people? That's what I want to know! Think of all those poor, innocent people, and all those children!

83

George: What about the depression? Now that was horrible. We nearly starved! What was He thinking to let Hoover get elected?

Shirley: How about cancer? I mean, I wouldn't even be here yet if it weren't for cancer! Look at all the suffering that causes!

Ida: You know, I think I'll ask Him about abortion. I never could make my mind up on that one.

Shirley: And euthanasia …

Ida: And the ozone layer …

George: And T. V. preachers …

Shirley: And drug abuse …

Ida: And child abuse …

George: And Republicans …

Shirley: And evolution …

Ida: There are so many questions.

Shirley: So many.

Ida: Well, I think He owes us some answers!

Shirley: Me, too!

George: And I'm going to get them!

Shirley: We'll all stand up to Him together. *(They all clasp hands in unity.)*

Ida: After all, it wasn't easy living on earth all those years.

Shirley: My neighbor, Mrs. Hardy, used to say, "Oh God's in control, God's in control." Well, if He was in control, why couldn't He do something about the bad things in the world?

George: Our pastor told us that God cared about everyone, but it sure didn't look that way to me. He didn't seem to care about my sister when she got

polio, or my mother when she nearly died from pneumonia in '34.

Ida: You know, it makes you wonder what He's been up to all these centuries. Why, it's downright cruel, some of the things He's done. Have you read the Old Testament?

George: Awful, isn't it? All that killing. I just don't understand it. But now we'll get some answers!

Ida: He's got a lot of explaining to do, if you ask me!

Shirley: Viet Nam!

George: Watergate!

Shirley: Pornography!

Ida: AIDS!

George: Nixon!

*The **Angel** enters during the previous exchange.*

Angel: *(clears throat)* Um … excuse me!
George, Ida, Shirley — right this way, please.

*The **Angel** motions them toward the front of the stage, where they stand side by side. The stage lights suddenly become extremely bright, or the actors may be lit by a very bright spotlight from the rear of the auditorium. They stare out above the audience in stupefaction, mouths hanging open, as if trying to speak, but can't. Then, one by one, they fall to their faces in worship. It is important to convey the idea that they are **worshipping** God, rather than merely cowering in fear.*

Blackout.

Optional: *In the darkness, read Revelation 15:4, Romans 9:20a, Zechariah 2:13, or other related Scripture.* **Song:** "Every Knee Shall Bow" *sung by Twila Paris works well at the end.*

THE BRIDE

by Susan Stimson

Purpose: *To show how we sometimes react in our relationship to God, although we are His children, and we as the church are the bride of Christ.*

Cast:
Bride
Groom
Preacher

*The scene opens with the **Bride** and **Groom** coming up the aisle to the **Preacher** and stopping in front of him.*

Preacher: I now pronounce you husband and wife.

The couple now turns to the audience.

Bride: You can take me home now, Dear.

Groom: Home. Oh no, we're going on our honeymoon.

Bride: Oh! I don't mean your home, I mean to *my* home. Take me back to my mom and dad.

Groom: What are you talking about, Dear? Did you forget something?

Bride: No, since we are married I'll try to be with you each week if it doesn't interfere with my plans. I like my life the way it has always been.

Groom: Wait a second! Don't you love me?

Bride: Of course I love you. I married you, didn't I? If something comes up, if I get sick, or need more money, or something I can't handle, I will call you right away.

Groom: Aren't you going to be living with me?

Bride: No! But I know you love me. Thank you for making me your own, but let's not go overboard with this. Let's not take this marriage business too seriously.

***Bride** and **Groom** leave and the **Preacher** begins the sermon.*

THE BIRTHDAY TREASURE

by Christy Doyle

Use this sketch as you celebrate Independence Day

Cast: *Jack and Char*

Setting: *Jack and Char are on an archeological dig.
They are dressed in casual clothes as they sift through dirt.*

Char: Oh, Jack, isn't this exhilarating?

Jack: *(coughing as he sifts dirt)* Yeah, this is how I planned on spending my summer vacation — rolling in dirt and manure. Some vacation!

Char: It's a wonderful vacation. I've always wanted to go on an archeological dig. It's so exciting.

Jack: Exciting? Yeah, I've always wanted to spend time with bugs, earthworms, and old broken vases that belonged to someone's great grandmother.

Char: But, Jack, this is history.

Jack: Can't we wait until it's on display in an air conditioned museum?

Char: But we might discover an important piece of history. Oh, it's so wonderful. It's like looking for buried treasure.

Jack: The only treasure I want to find is an airline ticket to a real vacation. Why can't we be like normal people and go to Disneyland?

Char: Jack, how can you compare finding a two hundred year old bone with Mickey Mouse?

Jack: You're right, Char. They're both so exciting I don't know if I can choose. . . fun and excitement on a thousand different rides is great, but I'm so tempted by spending eight hours in a mudhole with the sun beating down on my neck.

Char: You know you have to spend hours in the sun in line at Disneyland, too . . . and it's all forgotten in a few days. But a trip like this you never forget.

Jack: You got that right. I'll never forget this fourth day of July. If it weren't your birthday, I wouldn't be here.

Char: This is how everyone should spend this Fourth of July . . . Looking for a piece of history from our Christian forefathers.

Jack: They're not *my* Christian forefathers.

Char: Yes, they are.

Jack: No, they're not.

Char: Yes, they are.

Jack: Char, I've got one father and he's married to my mother and he's not a Christian.

Char: I'm talking about our Christian heritage. Just think, George Washington might have walked right here.

Jack: Yeah, but I bet he didn't have to spend his vacation here.

Char: You have no sense of history.

Jack: Yes, I do.

Char: No, you don't.

Jack: Char, when you told me that we were going to Virginia for the Fourth, I thought we'd be on a tour, not tramping in the dirt.

Char: But it's not just dirt.

Jack: Well, you could have fooled me.

Char: Jack, the Christian founders of our country lived here, and died here.

Jack: Yeah, and it smells like it, too.

Char: Okay, so it's not the normal vacation. But it's such a history lesson. How many people do you think know that Christopher Columbus was a Bible scholar?

Jack: Yeah, and how many people care?

Char: I care . . . What does the Fourth of July mean to you?

Jack: A barbeque, fireworks, and a case of beer — not necessarily in that order.

Char: You see? That's awful!!

Jack: It sounds pretty good to me.

Char: But it's awful that we've forgotten the real meaning. This country was founded as "one nation under God." If you do any kind of research you know that the first Americans believed that God sent them here. They were being led of God. They were filled with the Spirit.

Jack: Filled with a spirit? Whoa . . . that's spooky. Time to call Ghostbusters.

Char: No, Jack, filled with the Holy Spirit! . . . the Spirit of Jesus. They were serving their king . . . king Jesus.

Jack: Yeah, I'm devoted to the big king.

Char: (Getting excited) Why, Jack . . .

Jack: "Burger King" . . . Speaking of serving, is it almost lunch time yet?

Char: Okay, Jack, we'll go eat. I'm pretty hungry too. I guess I should thank the Lord for fast food.

Jack: (looking through his dirt) Hey, what's this? (He holds up a tiny cross.)

Char: Oh, Jack, it's a gold cross!

Jack: Yep, it's gold all right.

Char: You see! I can't believe how special this is.

Jack: It's special alright.

Char: We've found something very important . . . maybe even major. Who knows who has touched this?

Jack: How about the lady in the gift shop?

Char: What?

Jack: Yeah, it's your birthday present.

Char: My birthday present?

Jack: It's from the gift shop. I thought it would be fun to give it to you this way.

Char: *(disappointed)* Oh, Jack, that's awful!!

Jack: No, it's not! It's 18k gold.

Char: Oh, Jack, for one brief moment I thought I'd be part of history. I thought we had discovered this wonderful link between us and our Christian forefathers. I thought "Wow, what a wonderful present on our country's birthday and on my birthday."

Jack: It is a great present. This is 18k gold, you know, not 14k gold! The woman in the gift shop said it's the best cross they had. It was expensive, too.

Char: A gold cross!! Oh, Jack, how stupid can I be?

Jack: Oh, that's OK, Char, you didn't know it was expensive.

Char: No, you bought me a cross!

Jack: It took you long enough. I think this sun is slowing down your reactions.

Char: Jack, this is the first time you ever bought me something religious.

Jack: Do you like it?

Char: I love it! I can't believe that you actually went into a store and bought me a cross. You finally realize how important Jesus, my Savior and King, is to me.

Jack: Speaking of kings, I'm starved. Can we find that Burger King now?

Char: Sure, Jack. Oh, this is the best birthday *and* the best Fourth of July I've ever had!

Jack: Yeah, maybe next Fourth of July we could go on another dig.

Char: Another dig? Really, Jack?

Jack: Yeah, maybe we could "dig" a few sand castles at the beach . . . you "dig?"

Char: Yeah, I "dig."

They exit laughing.

CRUISIN'

by Matt Tullos

Cast:
#1 & #3: Enthusiastic travelers
#2: Skeptical traveler

Setting: *Four folding chairs in a car formation.*

#1: Hey look! A new car!

#3: It's got my name on it!

#2: What are we waiting for?

#3: Let's go!

#1: Wow! This is great! Five speed, cruise control, seven speaker stereo—

#2: What's that?

#3: Road sign

#1: It's the interstate! Hit the fast lane!

#2: You really think we should?

#3: Why not?

#1: Everybody takes the interstate.

#2: Everybody?

#1: Trust me!

#3: Would you look at that! Look at the destinations! Keg Parties! Music!

#2: Hey, check out that billboard!

#1: Everybody's having a blast!

#3: We're cruisin' now!

#2: Wait just a second. I thought I saw some drivers heading off the exit ramp. Look— they're heading in another direction.

#3: I think they're heading down the narrow road. Believe me. We've got too much horse power to bother leaving the interstate.

#2: It says, "For the ride of a lifetime, follow me!"

#1: If you took that road it **would** be a life-time! A lifetime of commitment and hard work. But it's better to burn out than to fade away. Right?!

#3: Plus, if we want to, we can always turn around and go back. We've got plenty of time.

#2: I guess you're right.

#1: Whoa! What's that!?

#2: I think our engine blew out!

#3: *(sarcastically)* Oh great. That's just great.

They get out of the car and mime opening the hood.

#1: Yuck! This smoke is the pits!

They talk to an imaginary person who has just walked up.

#2: Oh, Hi. *(pause)* Yeah. We could sure use some help. You see we were just going down the —

#3: Oh, so you saw the whole thing, huh?

#1: I think I've seen you somewhere before. Aren't you from the narrow road. *(pause)* You built it? So you do vehicle repair and restoration huh? Sounds like a lot of work.

Pause.

#3: No actually we're fine here. We really aren't interested in that kind of help. *(pause)* No, you don't understand. We like to do the driving ourselves.

#2: But we could just. . .

#3: *(to #2)* Look, if you don't want to go with us, find your own car.

#1: *(to imaginary person)* You want us to cruise with You? What? You think we can't cruise on our own?

#3: This car can't hold anymore.

#1: Hey, Mister, I think I see somebody else coming to help. Thanks for the offer. But right now, we want the fast lane on the interstate.

#2: Sure, I'll take your business card. JC's auto repair. Catchy name.

#1: Maybe we'll take you up on that one day.

#3: We'll have plenty of time to change our mind if things don't work out.

#2: See you later.

They look at a second imaginary person.

#3: Hey! How's it going. Wow! Now this is what I call service.

#1: Nice horns, buddy! You really look good in red.

Pause.

#2: You mean the car runs better if you floor it?

#1: Sounds fun to me.

#2: I don't know about this.

#3: You're finished already?

#1: Let's go!

#3: This is great. That guy must have done something to the fuel line! We're in warp drive.

#1: I can feel the G forces!

#2: There's a danger sign! Watch out!

#3: This is great! I love it!

#2: Cliff ahead! Don't you see that?!

#3: Loosen up! We're doing great, and plus, if we have to stop we've got

#1 & #3: Plenty of time!

#2: Hey! Look out!

#3: Hit the brakes!

#1: They're locked!

#2: Why didn't I —

All: AHHHH!!

TO REGIONS BEYOND

by Robert Allen

Where is the mission field?

Cast:
Tim Bradley
Sarah Bradley
Elsie Pendergast

Setting: *The scene takes place in the church lobby where* **Mrs. Pendergast** *has just caught up with the* **Bradleys**, *a young missionary couple.*

Elsie: Oh, there you are. Tim and Sarah Bradley, right?

Tim: That's right. And you?

Elsie: Mrs. Elsie Pendergast, but everyone calls me Mrs. P. Oh, it is so exciting to hear that you are going to be missionaries.

Sarah: Yes, we're quite excited about it ourselves. It's something we've known for a long time that God wanted us to do.

Elsie: Called of God. What a wonderful expression. I think foreign missions must be just about the most exciting thing God ever calls anyone to do.

Tim: Well, there is a great need all around the world.

Elsie: Oh, yes, but especially in those exotic places like Pango Pango and Bali Hai and the dark continent. Have you ever been to the dark continent, Mrs. Bradley?

Sarah: As a matter of fact we have.

Elsie: Oh, what stories you must have to tell. I could listen to missionary stories for hours. All the starvation and the wild animals and the savages shooting at everyone. Do you have a family?

Tim: Two wonderful children, a boy and a girl.

Elsie: And you're going to raise them on foreign soil. What dedication. So, when do you leave? When do you take off for the regions beyond? The dark continent? Egypt? Nigeria? South Africa?

Sarah: Oh, but you don't understand. We're on the mission field already.

Tim: We're *from* South Africa, Mrs. Pendergast. We have been sent here as missionaries to the United States.

THE KNOCK

By Darrell C. Cook

Cast: *Readers #1, #2, and Voice*

#1: To knock is to communicate.

#2: To knock is to worship.

#1: He knocks …

Voice: "Here I am! I stand at the door and knock. If anyone hears my voice and opens the door, I will come in and eat with him, and he with me." *(Rev. 3:20, NIV)*

#2: His knock assures me that He is there.

#1: His knock lets me know that He wants to spend time with me.

#2: His knock shows me that it is time to listen.

#1: To knock is to communicate.

#2: To knock is to worship.

#1: I knock …

Voice: "Ask and it will be given to you; seek and you will find; knock and the door will be opened to you. For everyone who asks receives; he who seeks finds; and to him who knocks, the door will be opened." *(Matt: 7:7-8, NIV)*

#2: My knock tells Him some things that He already knows — that I have a need.

#1: My knock tells the world that I know that He is there.

#2: My knock proclaims that I believe in His ability to meet needs.

#1: To knock is to communicate.

#2: To knock is to worship.

BOXES

By Tim Shamburger

Cast: Readers #1, #2, #3, and #4

#1: Boxes…

#2: Boxes can be made of many different materials, but most are cardboard.

#3: Boxes can be in a lot of shapes, but most are square.

#4: Boxes can be used for a lot of things.

#1: I like boxes that have presents inside!

#2: I like boxes that have food inside!

#3: I like boxes for storing things.

#4: I like boxes for carrying things.

#1: I really like boxes on moving day.

#2: Boxes also come in handy when you are mailing things.

#3: Boxes can be turned sideways for book-shelves.

#4: I like boxes for packing canned goods.

#1: Packing canned goods?

#4: Yeah, packing canned goods.

#1: Why in the world would you want to pack canned goods?

#4: Well, some people use boxes like these to pack canned goods to send to disaster areas, after a hurricane or flood.

#2: He's right, and when those boxes reach the disaster area, and the food is removed, some of the same people who get canned goods from the boxes, may use the boxes as umbrellas.

#3: Some might use them for a fire on a stormy night.

#4: Or as a safe place for the remaining things they own.

#1: Worst of all …

#2: Some people in the United States might be *living* in boxes even now.

#3: Give to the mission efforts of our church, and give *more* than boxes.

INDEX AND CALENDAR SUGGESTIONS

SCRIPTURE REFERENCES

These scriptures are directly quoted.